SA
POR
(Brazilian Usage)

BY

M. M. MICKLE

AND

FRANCISCO DA COSTA

DOVER PUBLICATIONS, INC.
NEW YORK

CONTENTS

Standard Book Number: 486-20809-5

Library of Congress Catalog Card Number: 57-22830

Manufactured in the United States of America

SCHEME OF PRONUNCIATION

The Portuguese typical of São Paulo and Southern Brazil is used as the basic pronunciation for this manual, since it is probably more easily imitated by Americans than the other dialects of this country. Although there are regional differences, you will be understood in all parts of Brazil as well as in Portugal and Portuguese territories if you use this pronunciation. The intention is to facilitate learning and imitating spoken Portuguese rather than to indicate phonetics with meticulous accuracy.

Portuguese vowels are pure, consisting of one sound only. They should be pronounced distinctly and not drawled as in English.

The pronunciation given should be read as in English, with the stress placed on the syllable in capital letters. A loop under the line indicates that the sounds thus connected are pronounced in one breath (e.g., *EHoo* for the Portuguese word *eu*). Since, in some cases, the pronunciation of a group of letters differs according to the English word in which it is found, and since a few Portuguese sounds cannot be represented in English, the following rules should be remembered:

    ah—like broad *a* in *father*.
    ay—like *ay* in *day*.
    aw—like *aw* in *paw*.
  dyoh—like *dee⁀oh* in one breath.
    ee—like *ee* in *bee*.
    eh—like *e* in *met*.
   ess—like *ess* in *less*.
   ew—like *ew* in *yew*.
g or *gh*—like *g* in *garden*.
    ie—like *i* in *ice*.
   oh—like *o* in *note*.
   oo—like *oo* in *moon*.
   ow—like *ow* in *now*.
   oy—like *oy* in *boy*.
    r—slightly trilled; flip the tongue against the gums of
      the upper teeth.
   rr—more strongly trilled.
 ryoh—like *ree⁀oh* pronounced in one breath.
s or *ss*—like *s* in *so*.
 syoh—like *see⁀oh* pronounced in one breath.
   zh—like *s* in *pleasure*.

NASAL SOUNDS

Special attention must be given to imitating nasal sounds in spoken Portuguese, since they cannot be represented in English. The breath passes through the mouth and the nose at the same time when nasal sounds are pronounced. The tongue and teeth should not move. A dash above letters always indicates nasalization in the phonetic transcription. In a few cases where the natural tendency of an American would be to nasalize, the dash has been omitted for the sake of simplicity and at no loss of comprehensibility.

    a̅h—like *a* in *father* nasalized.
    a̅y—like *ay* in *day* nasalized.
    e̅e—like *ee* in *bee* nasalized.
    e̅h—like *e* in *met* nasalized.
    i̅e—like *i* in *ice* nasalized.
    o̅h—like *o* in *note* nasalized.
    o̅o—like *oo* in *moon* nasalized.
    o̅w—like *ow* in *now* nasalized.
    o̅y—like *oy* in *boy* nasalized.

USEFUL EXPRESSIONS
EXPRESSÕES ÚTEIS

1. Yes. No. Perhaps.
Sim. Não. Talvez.
see. now. tahl-VAYSS.

2. Please ——.
Faça o favor de ——.
FAH-sah oh fah-VOHR day ——.

3. Excuse me? (Please repeat.)
Como?
KOH-moh?

4. Pardon me. (Forgive me.)
Desculpe.
days-KOOL-pay.

5. Thanks (very much).
(Muito) obrigado.
(MOO⏑een-toh) oh-bree-GAH-doh.

6. Don't mention it.
De nada.
day NAH-dah.

7. Do you speak English?
O senhor fala inglês?
oh say-NYOR FAH-lah een-GLAYSS?

8. I speak only English (French).
Eu falo só inglês, (francês).
eh⏑oo FAH-loh saw een-GLAYSS, (frahn-SAYSS).

5

9. German, Italian.
Alemão, italiano.
ah-lay-MŌW.   ee-tah-LYAH-noh.

10. I am from the United States.
Sou dos Estados Unidos.
soh dohss ess-TAH-dohss oo-NEE-dohss.

11. My (mailing) address is ——.
Meu enderêço (para cartas) é ——.
may͜oo en-deh-RAY-soh (PAH-rah KAHR-tahss) eh ——.

12. He (She) is from ——.
Êle, (ela) é de ——.
AY-lay, (EH-lah) eh day ——.

13. Please speak (more) slowly.
Fale (mais) devagar, por favor.
FAH-lay (MAH͜ees) day-vah-GAHR, pohr fah-VOHR.

14. I (do not) understand.
(Não) compreendo.
(now) kohm-pray-EN-doh.

15. Repeat it, please.
Repita, por favor.
ray-PEE-tah, pohr fah-VOHR.

16. Again.
Outra vez.
OH-trah vayss.

17. Write it down, please.
Escreva-o, por favor.
ess-CREH-vah-oh, pohr fah-VOHR.

18. What do you wish?
Que deseja?
kay day-ZAY-zhah?

19. How much is it?
Quanto é?
KWAHN-toh eh?

20. Come in. Come here.
Entre. Venha cá.
EN-tray. VAY-nyah kah.

21. Wait a moment.
Espere um momento.
ess-PEH-ray oo moh-MEN-toh.

22. Why? When?
Por que? Quando?
pohr kay? KWAHN-doh?

23. How? How long?
Como? Quanto tempo?
KOH-moh? KWAN-toh TEM-poh?

24. How far is ——?
A que distância fica ——?
ah kay dees-TAHN-syah FEE-kah ——?

25. Who? What?
Quem? Que?
kay? kay?

26. Where is (are) ——?
Onde está (estão) ——?
OHN-day ess-TAH (ess-TOW) ——?

27. Ladies' room.
O toalete de senhoras.
oh twah-LEH-tay day say-NYOH-rahss.

28. Men's room.
O toalete de homens.
oh twah-LEH-tay day OH-mayss.

29. Here, there.
Aquí, alí.
ah-KEE, ah-LEE.

30. It is (not) all right.
(Não) está bem.
(now) ess-TAH bay.

31. It is (old, new).
É (velho, novo).
eh (VEHL-yoh, NAW-voh).

32. Empty, full.
Vazio, cheio.
vah-ZEE-oh, SHAY-yoh.

33. That is (not) all.
(Não) é só.
(now) eh saw.

34. To, from, with.
A, de, com.
ah, day, koh.

35. In, on, near, far.
Em, sôbre, perto, longe.
ay, SOH-bray, PEHR-toh, LOHN-zhay.

36. In front of, behind.
Em frente de, atrás de.
$\overline{ay}$ *FREN-tay day, ah-TRAHSS day.*

37. Beside, inside, outside.
Ao lado de, dentro de, fora de.
ow LAH-doh day, DEN-troh day, FAW-rah day.

38. Several, few.
Vários, poucos.
VAH-ryohs, POH-kohss.

39. More, less.
Mais, menos.
MAH‿eess, MEH-nohss.

40. A little.
Um pouco.
$\overline{oo}$ *POH-koh.*

41. Enough, too much.
Suficiente, demais.
soo-fee-SYEN-tay, deh-MAH‿eess.

42. Much, many.
Muito, muitos.
MOO‿een-toh, MOO‿een-tohss.

43. Something, nothing.
Algo, nada.
AHL-goh, NAH-dah.

44. Good, better (than).
Bom, melhor (do que).
$\overline{boh}$, *mehl-YOHR (doh kay).*

45. Bad, worse (than).
Mau, pior (do que).
mow, pee-OHR (doh kay).

46. (Right) now.
Agora (mesmo).
ah-GOH-rah (MEHZ-moh).

47. Soon, later.
Cêdo, mais tarde.
SAY-doh, MAH_eess TAHR-day.

48. As soon as possible.
Tão cêdo como seja possível.
tow SAY-doh KOH-moh SAY-zhah poh-SEE-vehl.

49. At the latest.
O mais tardar.
oh MAH_eess tahr-DAHR.

50. At least.
Pelo menos.
PEH-loh MEH-nohss.

51. It is (too) late.
É (muito) tarde.
eh (MOO_een-toh) TAHR-day.

52. It is early.
É cêdo.
eh SAY-doh.

53. Slowly, slower.
Devagar, mais devagar.
day-vah-GAHR, MAH_eess day-vah-GAHR.

54. Quickly, faster.
Depressa, mais depressa.
deh-PREH-sah, MAH_eess deh-PREH-sah.

55. I am (not) in a hurry.
(Não) estou com pressa.
(now) ess-TOH koh PREH-sah.

56. I am warm (cold).
Estou com calor (frio).
ess-TOH koh kah-LOHR (FREE-oh).

57. I am hungry (thirsty, sleepy).
Estou com fome (sêde, sono).
ess-TOH koh FOH-may (SAY-day, SOH-noh).

58. I am busy (tired, ill).
Estou ocupado (cansado, doente).
ess-TOH oh-koo-PAH-doh (kahn-SAH-doh, doh-EN-tay).

59. What is the matter?
O que há?
oh kay ah?

60. Help! Fire! Thief!
Socorro! Incêndio! Ladrão!
soh-KOH-rroh! een-SEN-dyoh! lah-DROW!

61. Be careful!
Cuidado!
kwee-DAH-doh!

62. Listen. Look here.
Escute. Olhe.
ess-KOO-tay. OHL-yay.

63. Can you help me?
Pode ajudar-me, por favor?
*PAW-day   ah-zhoo-DAHR-may,   pohr   fah-
VOHR?*

64. I am looking for ——.
Estou procurando ——.
ess-TOH proh-koo-RAHN-doh ——.

65. I should like ——.
Gostaria de ——.
gaws-tah-REE-ah day ——.

66. Can you recommend a ——?
Pode recomendar um ——?
PAW-day ray-koh-men-DAHR o͞o ——?

67. Do you want ——?
Deseja ——?
day-ZAY-zhah ——?

68. I am (very) glad.
Estou (muito) contente.
ess-TOH (MOO‿een-toh) kohn-TEN-tay.

69. I am sorry.
Sinto muito.
SEEN-toh MOO‿een-toh.

70. It is (not) my fault.
Eu (não) tenho a culpa.
EH‿oo (no͞w) TAY-nyoh ah KOOL-pah.

71. Whose fault is it?
   De quem é a culpa?
   day $\overline{kay}$ *eh ah KOOL-pah?*

72. I (do not) know.
   (Não) sei.
   (now) say.

73. I think (so, not).
   Acho que (sim, não).
   AH-shoh kay (see, now).

74. What is that for?
   Para que é isso?
   PAH-rah kay eh EE-soh?

75. What is that called in Portuguese?
   Como se chama isso em português?
   KOH-moh say SHAH-mah EE-soh $\overline{ay}$ *pohr-too-*
      GAYSS?

76. How do you say ——?
   Como se diz ——?
   KOH-moh say deess ——?

77. How do you spell ——?
   Como se escreve ——?
   KOH-moh say ess-KREH-vay ——?

DIFFICULTIES
DIFICULDADES

80. I cannot find my hotel address.
   Não posso achar o endereço de meu hotel.
   now PAW-soh ah-SHAHR oh en-day-RAY-soh
      day MAY͜oo oh-TEHL.

81. I do not remember the street.

Não me lembro da rua.

nãow may LEM-broh dah ROO-ah.

82. I have lost my friends.

Perdí meus amigos.

pehr-DEE MAY‿ooss ah-MEE-gohss.

83. I left my purse (wallet) in the ——.

Dexei minha bolsa, (carteira) no ——.

day-SHAY MEE-nyah BOHL-sah, (kahr-TAY-rah) noh ——.

84. I forgot my money (my key).

Esquecí meu dinheiro (minha chave).

ess-kay-SEE MAY‿oo dee-NYAY-roh, (MEE-nyah SHAH-vay).

85. I have missed my (train, plane).

Perdí meu (trem, avião).

pehr-DEE MAY‿oo (trãy, ah-vee-OW).

86. What am I to do?

Que devo fazer?

kay DAY-voh fah-ZEHR?

87. You said it would cost ——.

O senhor disse que custaria ——.

oh say-NYOHR DEE-say kay kooss-tah-REE-ah ——.

88. They are bothering us (me).

Êles estão nos (me) incomodando.

AY-layss es-TOW nohss (may) een-koh-maw-DAHN-doh.

89. Go away.
Vá embora.
vah em-BAW-rah.

90. I will call a policeman.
Chamarei um guarda.
shah-mah-RAY oo GWAHR-dah.

91. I have been robbed of ——.
Roubaram meu ——.
roh-BAH-row MAY oo ——.

92. Where is the police station?
Onde fica a delegacia de polícia?
OHN-day FEE-kah ah deh-lay-gah-SEE-ah day poh-LEE-syah?

93. The lost and found desk.
O departamento de perdidos e achados.
oh day-pahr-tah-MEN-toh day pehr-DEE-dohss ee ah-SHAH-dohss.

GREETINGS AND INTRODUCTIONS
SAUDAÇÕES E APRESENTAÇÕES

94. Good morning *or* **Good day.**
Bom dia.
boh DEE-ah.

95. Good afternoon.
Bôa tarde.
BOH-ah TAHR-day.

96. Good night.
Bôa noite.
BOH-ah NOY-tay.

97. Good-by. Until next time.

Adeus.   Até logo.

ah-DAY‿ooss. ah-TAY LAW-goh.

98. My name is ——.

Meu nome é ——.

MAY‿oo NOH-may eh ——.

99. What is your name?

Como é o seu nome?

KOH-moh eh oh SAY‿oo NOH-may?

100. May I introduce Mr. ——, Miss ——, Mrs. ——.

Apresento o senhor ——, a senhorita ——, a senhora ——.

ah-pray-ZEN-toh oh say-NYOHR ——, ah say-nyoh-REE-tah ——, ah say-NYOH-rah ——.

101. My wife, my husband.

Minha espôsa, meu marido.

MEE-nyah ess-POH-zah, MAY‿oo mah-REE-doh.

102. My daughter, my son.

Minha filha, meu filho.

MEE-nyah FEEL-yah, MAY‿oo FEEL-yoh.

103. My (lady) friend, my (man) friend.

Minha amiga, meu amigo.

MEE-nyah ah-MEE-gah, MAY‿oo ah-MEE-goh.

104. My sister, my brother.
Minha irmã, meu irmão.
MEE-nyah eer-MAH, MAY͜ oo eer-MOW.

105. I am very glad to meet you.
Muito prazer.
MOO͜ een-toh prah-ZEHR.

106. The pleasure is mine.
Igualmente.
ee-gwahl-MEN-tay.

107. How are you?
Como vai?
KOH-moh vie?

108. Fine.   And you?
Muito bem.   E o senhor, (a senhora)?
MOO͜ een-toh bay.   ee oh say-NYOHR, (ah say-NYAW-rah)?

109. How is your family?
Como vai a sua familia?
KOH-moh vie ah SOO-ah fah-MEE-lyah?

110. Not very well.
Não muito bem.
now MOO͜ een-toh bay.

111. Please sit down.
Sente-se, por favor.
SEN-tay-say, pohr fah-VOHR.

112. I have enjoyed myself very much.
Gostei muito.   Muito obrigado.
gawss-TAY MOO͜ een-toh.   MOO͜ een-toh oh-bree-GAH-doh.

113. I hope to see you again soon.

Espero vê-lo outra vez brevemente.

ess-PEH-roh VAY-loh OH-trah vayss breh-vay-MEN-tay.

114. Come (to see me, to see us).

Venha (visitar-me, visitar-nos).

VAY-nyah (vee-zee-TAHR-may, vee-zee-TAHR-nohss).

115. Are you free (this afternoon, this evening)?

Tem compromisso para (esta tarde, esta noite)?

tay kohm-proh-MEE-soh PAH-rah (ESS-tah TAHR-day, ESS-tah NOY-tay)?

116. Please give me (your address, telephone number).

Dê-me (o seu enderêço, o número do seu telefone), por favor.

DAY-may (oh SAY‿oo en-day-RAY-soh, oh NOO-may-roh doh SAY‿oo teh-lay-FOH-nay) pohr fah-VOHR.

117. Give my regards to ——.

Lembranças a ——.

lem-BRAHN-sahss ah ——.

118. I am (we are) going to ——.

Vou (vamos) a ——.

voh (VAH-mohss) ah ——.

TRAVEL
A VIAGEM

General Expressions—Expressões gerais

120. Where is ——?
Onde fica ——?
OHN-day FEE-kah ——?

121. I want to go to the airline office for ——.
Desejo ir ao escritório da linha aérea para ——.
day-ZAY-zhoh eer ow ess-kree-TAW-ryoh dah LEE-nyah ah-AY-ray-ah PAH-rah ——.

122. The airport
O aeroporto.
oh ah-AY-roh-POHR-toh.

123. The bus station.
A estação de ônibus.
ah ess-tah-SOW day OH-nee-booss.

124. The dock.
A doca.
ah DAW-kah.

125. The railroad station.
A estação de trens.
ah ess-tah-SOW day trayss.

126. The ticket office.
A bilheteria.
ah beel-yay-tay-REE-ah.

127. A ticket, a time-table.
Um bilhete, um horário.
oo beel-YAY-tay, oo oh-RAH-ryoh.

128. A (baggage) porter.
Um carregador.
oo kah-rray-gah-DOHR.

129. The baggage room.
O depósito de bagagem.
oh day-PAW-zee-toh day bah-GAH-zhay.

130. The platform.
A plataforma.
ah plah-tah-FOHR-mah.

131. How long will it take to go?
Quanto tempo precisa para chegar là?
KWAHN-toh TEM-poh pray-SEE-zah PAH-rah shay-GAHR lah?

132. When will we arrive at ——?
Quando chegaremos a ——?
KWAHN-doh shay-gah-RAY-mohss ah ——?

133. Please get me a taxi.
Chame um taxi, por favor.
SHAH-may oo TAHK-see, pohr fah-VOHR.

134. Is this seat taken?
Este lugar está ocupado?
AYSS-tay loo-GAHR ess-TAH oh-koo-PAH-doh?

135. Can I reserve a seat?
Posso reservar um assento?
PAW-soh ray-sehr-VAHR $\overline{oo}$ ah-SEN-toh?

136. A seat near the window.
Um assento perto da janela.
$\overline{oo}$ ah-SEN-toh PEHR-toh dah zhah-NEH-lah.

137. Is this the (direct) way to ——?
É êste o caminho (diréto) para ——?
eh AYSS-tay oh kah-MEE-nyoh (dee-REH-toh) PAH-rah ——?

138. How does one go to ——?
Como se vai a ——?
KOH-moh say vie ah ——?

139. Where do I turn?
Onde devo virar?
OHN-day DAY-voh vee-RAHR?

140. To the north, to the south.
Para o norte, para o sul.
PAH-rah oh NAWR-tay, PAH-rah oh sool.

141. From the east, from the west.
Do este, do oeste.
doh ESS-tay, doh oh-ESS-tay.

142. To the (left, right).
À (esquerda, direita).
ah (ess-KEHR-dah, dee-RAY-tah).

143. Straight ahead.
Diretamente em frente.
dee-reh-tah-MEN-tay $\overline{ay}$ FREN-tay.

144. Forward, back.
Para frente, para trás.
PAH-rah FREN-tay, PAH-rah trahss.

145. What street is this?
Que rua é esta?
kay ROO-ah eh ESS-tah?

146. Square, place.
Praça, lugar.
PRAH-sah, loo-GAHR.

147. Two blocks ahead.
A dois quarteirões daquí.
ah doyss kwahr-tay-RŌYSS dah-KEE.

148. Please point.
Faça o favor de apontar.
FAH-sah oh fah-VOHR day ah-pohn-TAHR.

149. Do I have to change?
Tenho que baldear?
TAY-nyoh kay bahl-day-AHR?

150. Please tell me where to get off.
Diga-me onde devo saltar, por favor.
*DEE-gah-may OHN-day day-voh sahl-TAHR,
pohr fah-VOHR.*

AT THE CUSTOMS
NA ALFÂNDEGA

152. Where is the customs?
Onde é a alfândega?
OHN-day eh ah ahl-FAHN-day-gah?

153. This is my baggage. —— pieces.
Esta é a minha bagagem. —— volumes.
ESS-tah eh ah MEE-nyah bah-GAH-zhay.
—— *voh-LOO-mayss.*

154. Here is my passport.
Aquí está meu passaporte.
ah-KEE ess-TAH MAY‿oo pah-sah-POHR-tay.

155. Shall I open everything?
Devo abrir tudo?
DAY-voh ah-BREER TOO-doh?

156. I cannot open that.
Não posso abrir essa.
now PAW-soh ah-BREER EH-sah.

157. I have lost the key.
Perdí a chave.
pehr-DEE ah SHAH-vay.

158. I have nothing to declare.
Não tenho nada a declarar.
now TAY-nyoh NAH-dah ah day-klah-RAHR.

159. All this is for personal use.
Tudo isto é de uso pessoal.
TOO-doh EESS-toh eh day OO-zoh peh-soh-AHL.

160. There is nothing here but ——.
Aquí não há mais do que ——.
ah-KEE now ah MAH‿eess doh kay ——.

161. These are gifts.

Êstes são presentes.

AYSS-tayss sōw pray-ZEN-tayss.

162. Are these things dutiable?

Precisa pagar direitos sôbre êstes artigos?

pray-SEE-zah   pah-GAHR   dee-RAY-tohss
SOH-bray AYSS-tayss ahr-TEE-gohss?

163. How much must I pay?

Quanto devo pagar?

KWAHN-toh DAY-voh pah-GAHR?

164. This is all I have.

Isto é tudo o que tenho.

EESS-toh eh TOO-doh oh kay TAY-nyoh.

165. Please be careful.

Tenha cuidado, por favor.

TAY-nyah kwee-DAH-doh, pohr fah-VOHR.

166. Have you finished?

Já acabou?

zhah ah-kah-BOH?

167. I cannot find my baggage.

Não posso encontrar minha bagagem.

nōw PAW-soh en-kohn-TRAHR MEE-nyah
bah-GAH-zhay.

168. My train leaves in —— minutes.

O meu trem sai em —— minutos.

oh MAY‿oo trāy sie āy —— mee-NOO-tohss.

TICKETS
OS BILHETES

170. How much is a ticket to ——?
Quanto custa um bilhete para ——?
KWAHN-toh KOO-stah $\overline{oo}$ beel-YAY-tay
PAH-rah ——?

171. One way ticket.
Um bilhete de ida.
$\overline{oo}$ beel-YAY-tay day EE-dah.

172. A round trip ticket.
Um bilhete de ida e volta.
$\overline{oo}$ beel-YAY-tay day EE-dah eh VOHL-tah.

173. First-class, second-class, third-class.
Primeira classe, segunda classe, terceira
classe.
pree-MAY-rah KLAH-say, say-GOON-dah
KLAH-say, tehr-SAY-rah KLAH-say.

174. Can I go by way of ——?
Posso ir via ——?
PAW-soh eer VEE-ah ——?

175. How long is it good for?
Por quanto tempo é válido?
pohr KWAHN-toh TEM-poh eh VAH-lee-
doh?

176. Can I get something to eat on the way?
Há restaurante no caminho?
ah ress-tow-RAHN-tay noh kah-MEE-nyoh?

177. How much baggage may I take?
Quantos kilos de bagagem posso levar
comigo?
KWAHN-tohss KEE-lohss day bah-GAH-
zhay PAW-soh leh-VAHR koh-MEE-goh?

178. How much per kilogram for excess?
Quanto se paga por kilo de excesso?
KWAHN-toh say PAH-gah pohr KEE-loh day
ayss-SEH-soh?

179. Is there travel insurance?
Há seguros de viagem para passageiros?
ah say-GOO-rohss day VYAH-zhay PAH-rah
pah-sah-ZHAY- rohss?

BAGGAGE
A BAGAGEM

181. Where is the baggage checked?
Onde se despacha a bagagem?
OHN-day say dayss-PAH-shah ah bah-GAH-
zhay?

182. I want to leave these bags for a while.
Desejo deixar estas maletas por um
momento.
day-ZAY-zhoh day-SHAR ESS-tahss mah-
LAY-tahss por oo moh-MEN-toh.

183. Do I pay now or later?
Pago agora ou depois?
PAH-goh ah-GOH-rah oh day-POYSS?

184. I want to take out my baggage.

Desejo retirar a minha bagagem.

day-ZAY-zhoh ray-tee-RAHR ah MEE-nyah bah-GAH-zhay.

185. That is mine there.

Aquela é minha.

ah-KEH-lah eh MEE-nyah.

186. Handle this very carefully.

Tenha muito cuidado com isto.

TAY-nyah MOO⌣een-toh kwee-DAH-doh koh EE-stoh.

TRAIN
O TREM

188. I am going by train to ——.

Eu vou de trem a ——.

EH⌣oo voh day tray ah ——.

189. At what platform is the train for ——?

Em que plataforma está o trem para ——?

ay kay plah-tah-FOHR-mah ess-TAH oh tray PAH-rah ——?

190. Is the train for —— on time?

O trem para —— está no horário?

oh tray PAH-rah ——ess-TAH noh oh-RAH-ryoh?

191. It is ten minutes late.

Está atrasado dez minutos.

ess-TAH ah-trah-ZAH-doh dehss mee-NOO-tohss.

192. Put this in the rack.
Ponha isto na prateleira.
POH-nyah EESS-toh nah prah-tah-LAY-rah.

193. Please close (open) the window.
Feche (abra) a janela, por favor.
FAY-shay (AH-brah) ah zhah-NEH-lah, pohr fah-VOHR.

194. Where is the (diner, the smoker)?
Onde está (o restaurante, a sala de fumar)?
OHN-day ess-TAH oh reh-stow-RAHN-tay, ah SAH-lah day foo-MAHR?

195. Do you mind my smoking?
Não a incomoda o fumo?
now ah een-koh-MOH-dah oh FOO-moh?

196. Can you give me a match?
Tem um fósforo?
tay oo FAWSS-foh-roh?

197. What time is breakfast?
A que hora é o café?
ah kay OH-rah eh oh kah-FEH?

AIRPLANE
O AVIÃO

199. Is there motor service to the airport?
Há serviço de condução para o aeropôrto?
ah sehr-VEE-syoh day kohn-doo-SOW PAH-rah oh ah- ay-roh-POHR-toh?

200. At what time will they come for me?
A que hora virão buscar-me?
ah kay OH-rah vee-ROW boos-KAHR-may?

201. Where is there a plane to ——?
Quando haverá avião para ——?
KWAHN-doh ah-veh-RAH ah-vee-OW PAH-rah ——?

202. Is food served on the plane?
Servem refeição no avião?
SEHR-vay ray-fay-SOW noh ah-vee-OW?

203. How much baggage may I take?
Quanto posso levar de bagagem?
KWAHN-toh PAW-soh leh-VAHR day bah-GAH-zhay?

BUS
O ÔNIBUS

205. How often do the buses go?
Qual é o horário dos ônibus?
kwahl eh oh oh-RAH-ryoh dohss OH-nee-booss?

206. Can I buy an excursion ticket?
Posso comprar um bilhete de excursão?
PAW-soh kohm-PRAHR oo beel-YAY-tay day ess-koor-SOW?

207. Is there a stop for lunch?
Há parada para almôço?
ah pah-RAH-dah PAH-rah ahl-MOH-soh?

208. Can one stop over on the way?
Pode-se fazer escala pelo caminho?
PAW-day-say fah-ZEHR ess-KAH-lah PEH-loh kah-MEE-nyoh?

BOAT
O NAVIO

210. Can one go by boat to ——?
Pode-se ir de navio a ——?
PAW-day-say eer day nah-VEE-oh ah ——?

211. When does the next boat leave?
Quando sairá o próximo navio?
KWAHN-doh sah-ee-RAH oh PRAWS-see-moh nah-VEE-oh?

212. When must I go on board?
Quando deverei ir para bordo?
KWAHN-doh day-veh-RAY eer PAH-rah BOHR-doh?

213. Can I land at ——?
Posso desembarcar em ——?
PAW-soh day-zem-bahr-KAHR $\overline{ay}$ ——?

214. Are meals served on the boat?
Servem refeições no navio?
SEHR-v$\overline{ay}$ ray-fay-S$\overline{OY}$SS noh nah-VEE-oh?

215. The captain, the purser.
O comandante, o comissário.
oh koh-mahn-DAHN-tay, oh koh-mee-SAH-ryoh.

216. The cabin steward, the deck.
O camaroteiro, o convés.
oh kah-mah-roh-TAY-roh, oh kohn-VEHSS.

217. I want to rent a deck chair.
Quero alugar uma cadeira de convés.
KEH-roh ah-loo-GAHR OO-mah kah-DAY-rah day kohn-VEHSS.

218. I am a little sea-sick.
Estou um pouco mareado.
ess-TOH oo POH-koh mah-ray-AH-doh.

219. I am going to my stateroom.
Vou ao meu camarote.
voh ow MAY‿oo kah-mah-RAW-tay.

220. Let's go to the (dining salon, lounge).
Vamos ao (salão de jantar, salão).
VAH-mohss ow (sah-LOW day zhahn-TAHR, sah-LOW).

221. A life boat, a life preserver.
Uma baleeira, um salva-vidas.
OO-mah bah-lay-AY-rah, oo SAHL-vah-VEE-dahss.

AUTOMOBILE MOTORING
AUTOMÓVEL

223. Can you recommend a mechanic?
Pode recomendar um mecânico?
PAW-day ray-koh-men-DAHR oo may-KAH-nee-koh?

224. Where is a (gas station, garage)?

Onde fica (um pôsto de gasolina, uma garage)?

OHN-day FEE-kah ($\overline{oo}$ POHSS-toh day gah-zoh-LEE-nah, OO-mah gah-RAH-zhay)?

225. Is the road good?

A estrada é bôa?

ah ess-TRAH-dah eh BOH-ah?

226. Is it hard or dirt surface?

Está asfaltada ou de terra?

ess-TAH ahss-fahl-TAH-dah oh day TEH-rrah?

227. What town is (this, the next one)?

Como se chama (esta cidade, a próxima cidade)?

KOH-moh say SHAH-mah (ESS-tah see-DAH-day, ah PRAWS-see-mah see-DAH-day?

228. Where does that road go?

Para onde vai essa estrada?

PAH-rah OHN-day vie EH-sah ess-TRAH-dah?

229. The tourist club.

O clube de turismo.

oh KLOO-bay day too-REEZ-moh.

230. I have an international driver's licence.

Tenho uma carta internacional de motorista.

TAY-nyoh OO-mah KAHR-tah een-tehr-nah-syoh-NAHL day moh-toh-REESS-tah.

231. I want some air.

Quero encher os pneus.

Keh-roh en-SHEHR ohss pay-NAY͜ooss.

232. How much is gas a liter?

Quanto é o litro de gasolina?

KWAHN-toh eh oh LEE-troh day gah-zoh-LEE-nah?

233. Give me —— liters.

Dê-me —— litros.

DAY-may —— LEE-trohss.

234. Please change the oil.

Mude o óleo, por favor.

MOO-day oh AW-lay-oh, pohr fah-VOHR.

235. (Light, medium, heavy) oil.

Óleo (leve, médio, pesado).

AW-lay-oh (LEH-vay, MEH-dyoh, peh-ZAH-doh).

236. Put water in the battery.

Ponha água no acumulador.

POH-nyah AH-gwah noh ah-koo-moo-lah-DOHR.

237. Can you lubricate the car?

Pode lubrificar o carro?

PAW-day loo-bree-fee-KAHR oh KAH-rroh?

238. Could you wash it (now, soon)?

Pode lavá-lo (agora, cêdo)?

PAW-day lah-VAH-loh (ah-GOH-rah, SAY-doh)?

239. Adjust the brakes.
Ajuste os freios.
ah-ZHOOSS-tay ohss FRAY-yohss.

240. Will you check the tires?
Quer examinar os pneus?
kehr eh-zah-mee-NAHR ohss pay-NAY‿ooss?

241. Can you fix the flat tire?
Pode encher o pneu vazio?
PAW-day en-SHEHR oh pay-NAY‿oo vah-ZEE-oh?

242. A punctured tire.   A slow leak.
Um pneu furado.   Um escape de ar.
ōō pay-NAY‿oo foo-RAH-doh.   ōō ess-KAH-pay day ahr.

243. The —— does not work well.
O —— não funciona bem.
oh —— nōw foon-SYOH-nah bāy.

244. What is wrong?
Que é que tem?
kay eh kay tāy?

245. There is a (grinding, leak, noise).
Há um (rangido, escape, barulho).
ah ōō (rahn-ZHEE-doh, ess-KAH-pay, bah-ROOL-yoh).

246. The engine overheats.
O motor esquenta demais.
oh moh-TOHR ess-KEN-tah deh-MAH‿eess.

247. It (skips, stalls).
   O motor (falha, pára).
   oh moh-TOHR (FAHL-yah, PAH-rah).

248. There is a (rattle, squeak).
   Há (uma batida, um chiado).
   ah (OO-mah bah-TEE-dah, oo shee-AH-do).

249. May I park here for a while?
   Posso estacionar o meu carro aqui por um
   momento?
   PAW-soh ess-TAH-syoh-NAHR oh MAY‿oo
   KAH-rroh ah-KEE pohr oo moh-MEN-toh?

250. I want to garage my car for the night.
   Quero deixar meu carro na garage
   durante a noite.
   KEH-roh day-SHAR MAY‿oo KAR-rroh
   nah gah-RAH-zhay doo-RAHN-tay ah
   NOY-tay.

251. When does it (open, close)?
   A que hora (abre, fecha)?
   ah kay OH-rah (AH-bray, FAY-shah)?

HELP ON THE ROAD
AJUDA DA ESTRADA

253. I am sorry to trouble you.
   Sinto muito incomodá-lo.
   SEEN-toh MOO‿een-toh een-koh-moh-DAH-
   loh.

254. My car has broken down.
 Meu carro está enguiçado.
 MAY‿oo KAH-rroh ess-TAH en-ghee-SAH-doh.

255. Can you (tow, push) me?
 Pode (rebocar, empurrar) meu carro?
 PAW-day (ray-boh-KAHR, em-poo-RRAHR) MAY‿oo KAH-rroh?

256. Can you help me jack up the car?
 Pode ajudar-me a levantar o carro com o macaco?
 PAW-day ah-zhoo-DAHR-may ah leh-vahn-TAHR oh KAH-rroh koh͞ oh mah-KAH-koh?

257. Will you help me put on the spare?
 Quer ajudar-me a pôr o pneu sobressalente?
 kehr ah-zhoo-DAHR-may ah pohr oh pay-NAY‿oo soh-bray-sah-LEN-tay?

258. Will you take me to a garage?
 Quer levar-me a uma garage?
 kehr leh-VAHR-may ah OO-mah gah-RAH-zhay?

259. Could you give me some gas?
 Pode dar-me um pouco de gasolina?
 PAW-day DAHR-may o͞o POH-koh day gah-zoh-LEE-nah?

260. Will you help me get the car off the road?

Quer ajudar-me a tirar o carro para fora da estrada?

kehr ah-zhoo-DAHR-may ah tee-RAHR oh KAH-rroh PAH-rah FAW-rah dah ess-TRAH-dah?

261. My car is stuck (in the mud).

Meu carro está atolado (na lama).

MAY⌣oo KAH-rroh ess-TAH ah-toh-LAH-doh (nah LAH-mah).

262. It is in the ditch.

Está na vala.

ess-TAH nah VAH-lah.

PARTS, TOOLS, AND EQUIPMENT
PEÇAS E ACESSÓRIOS

265. Accelerator. O acelerador.
oh ah-seh-leh-rah-DOHR.

266. Battery. O acumulador.
oh ah-koo-moo-lah-DOHR.

267. Bolt. O grampo. *oh GRAHM-poh.*

268. Nut. A rôsca. *ah ROHSS-kah.*

269. Brake. O freio. *oh FRAY-yoh.*

270. Engine. O motor. *oh moh-TOHR.*

271. Spring. A mola. *ah MAW-lah.*

272. Starter. A partida.
ah pahr-TEE-dah.

273. Steering wheel. A direção.
ah dee-reh-SŌW.

274. Head light. O farol. *oh fah-ROHL.*

275. Tail light. A luz traseira.
ah looss trah-ZAY-rah.

276. Tube. A câmara-de-ar.
ah KAH-mah-rah-day-ahr.

277. Tire. O pneu. *o pay-NAY‿oo.*

278. Spare tire. O pneu sobressalente.
oh pay-NAY‿oo soh-bray-sah-LEN-tay.

279. Wheel (front, back, left, right).
A roda (dianteira, traseira, esquerda, direita).
ah RAW-dah (dyahn-TAY-rah, trah-ZAY-rah, ess-KEHR-dah, dee-RAY-tah).

280. Chains. As correntes.
ahss koh-RREN-tayss.

281. Hammer. O martelo.
oh mahr-TEH-loh.

282. Jack. O macaco. *oh mah-KAH-koh.*

283. Key. A chave. *ah SHAH-vay.*

284. Pliers. O alicate. *oh ah-lee-KAH-tay.*

285. Rope. A corda. *ah KAWR-dah.*

286. Screwdriver. A chave de fenda.
ah SHAH-vay day FEN-dah.

287. Tire pump. A bomba. *ah BOHM-bah.*

288. Wrench. A chave inglêsa.
ah SHAH-vay een-GLAY-zah.

ROAD SIGNS AND PUBLIC NOTICES
AVISOS DE TRÁFEGO

This section has been alphabetized in Portuguese to facilitate the tourist's reading of road signs and notices.

290. Atenção! Trem! *ah-ten-SOW! tray!*
RR crossing.

291. Cabos de alta tensão.
KAH-bohss day AHL-tah ten-SOW.
High tension lines.

292. Caminho estreito.
kah-MEE-nyoh ess-TRAY-toh.
Narrow road.

293. Conserve-se à direita.
kohn-SEHR-vay-say ah dee-RAY-tah.
Keep right.

294. Cruzamento.
kroo-zah-MEN-toh.
Intersection.

295. Cuidado! *kwee-DAH-doh!*
Drive carefully!

296. Curva (à direita, à esquerda).
KOOR-vah (ah dee-RAY-tah, ah ess-KEHR-dah).
(Right, left) Curve.

297. Curva fechada.
KOOR-vah fay-SHAH-dah.
Sharp turn.

298. Descida.   *dehss-SEE-dah.*   **Dip.**

299. Descida muito inclinada.
    dehss-SEE-dah MOO‿een-toh een-klee-NAH-dah.
  Steep grade.

300. Desvio.   *dayss-VEE-oh.*   **Detour.**

301. Devagar.   *day-vah-GAHR.*
  Drive slowly.

302. Entrada.   *en-TRAH-dah.*   **Entrance.**

303. Entrada proibida.
    en TRAH-dah proy-BEE-dah.
  Keep out.

304. É proibido fumar.
    eh proy-BEE-doh foo-MAHR.
  No smoking.

305. Escola.   *ess-KAW-lah.*   **School.**

306. Estacionamento (Proibido).
    ess-tah-syoh-nah-MEN-toh (proy-BEE-doh).
  (No) Parking.

307. Estrada.
    ess-TRAH-dah.
  Road.

308. Fechado.   *fay-SHAH-doh.*   **Closed.**

309. Fim de estrada asfaltada.
    fee day ess-TRAH-dah ahss-fahl-TAH-dah.
  Pavement ends.

310. Homens.   *OH-mayss.*   **Men.**

311. Homens Trabalhando.
OH-māyss trah-bahl-YAHN-doh.
Men working.

312. Não entre (à direita, à esquerda).
now̄ EN-tray ah dee-RAY-tah, ah ess-KEHR-dah).
No (right, left) turn.

313. (Não, Nunca) páre na pista.
(now̄, NOON-kah) PÀH-ray nah PEES-tah.
(Do not, Never) stop on the highway.

314. Páre.   *PAH-ray.*   **Stop.**

315. Perigo.   *pay-REE-goh.*   **Danger.**

316. Ponte (estreita, provisória).
POHN-tay (ess-TRAY-tah, proh-vee-ZAW-ryah).
(Narrow, temporary) bridge.

317. Pôsto de Pedágio.
POHSS-toh day pay-DAH-zhyoh.
Toll station.

318. Proibida conversão à esquerda.
proy-BEE-dah kohn-vehr-SŌW ah ess-KEHR-dah.
No U turn.

319. Reduza a velocidade.
ray-DOO-zah ah vay-loh-SEE-dah-day.
Slow down.

320. Saída.   *sah-EE-dah.*   **Exit.**

321. Senhoras.   *say-NYAW-rahss.*   **Ladies.**

322. Siga.   *SEE-gah.*   **Go.**

323. Trânsito Impedido.
TRAHN-see-toh eem-peh-DEE-doh.
No thoroughfare.

325. Use a segunda.
OO-zay ah say-GOON-dah.
Use second gear.

326. Velocidade máxima —— kilômetros por
hora.
*veh-loh-see-DAH-day MAS-see-mah —— kee-
LOH-meh-trohss pohr OH-rah.*
Speed limit —— kilometers per hour.

STREETCAR AND LOCAL BUS
O BONDE E O ÔNIBUS LOCAL

328. The bus stop, ticket.
A parada de ônibus, o bilhete de passagem.
*ah pah-RAH-dah day OH-nee-boos, oh beel-
YAY-tay day pah-SAH-zhay.*

329. The conductor, driver.
O cobrador, o motorista.
oh koh-brah-DOHR, oh moh-toh-REESS-tah.

330. What bus (car) do I take for ——?
Que ônibus (bonde) devo tomar para
——?
*kay OH-nee-booss (BOHN-day) DAY-voh
toh-MAHR PAH-rah ——?*

331. Where does the bus for —— stop?

Onde pára o ônibus para ——?

OHN-day PAH-rah oh OH-nee-booss PAH-rah ——?

332. How much is the fare?

Quanto custa a passagem?

KWAHN-toh KOOSS-tah ah pah-SAH-shay?

333. Do you go near ——?

O senhor passa perto de ——?

oh SAY-nyohr PAH-sah PEHR-toh day ——?

334. Change here.   The next stop.

Baldeie aquí.   A próxima parada.

bahl-DAY-yay ah-KEE.   ah PRAWS-see-mah pah-RAH-dah.

335. Two blocks more.

Mais dois quarteirões.

MAH-eess doyss kwahr-tay-ROYSS.

TAXI

O TAXI

337. Please call me a taxi.

Chame um taxi, por favor.

SHAH-may oo TAHK-see, pohr fah-VOHR.

338. How far is it?

A que distância fica?

ah kay dees-TAHN-syah FEE-kah?

339. How much will it cost?
Quanto custará?
KWAHN-toh kooss-tah-RAH?

340. That is too much.
Isso é muito.
EE-soh eh MOO‿een-toh.

341. What do you charge an hour?
Quanto cobra por hora?
KWAHN-toh KOH-brah pohr OH-rah?

342. I just wish to drive around.
Quero só dar uma volta.
KEH-roh saw dahr OO-mah VOHL-tah.

343. Please drive slower.
Guie mais devagar, por favor.
GHEE-ay MAH-eess day-vah-GAHR pohr fah-VOHR.

344. Drive more carefully.
Guie com máis cuidado.
GHEE-ay koh̄ MAH‿ees kwee-DAH-doh.

345. Stop here.   Wait for me.
Pare aquí.   Espere por mim.
PAH-ray ah-KEE.   ess-PEH-ray pohr mēē.

346. (You can) go by way of ——.
Pode ir por ——.
PAW-day eer pohr ——.

347. How much do I owe you?
Quanto lhe devo?
KWAHN-toh yay day-voh?

LODGING
A HOSPEDAGEM

349. Which hotel is (good, inexpensive)?

Que hotel é (bom, barato)?

kay oh-TEHL eh (bo͞h, bah-RAH-toh)?

350. The best hotel.

O melhor hotel.

oh mehl-YOHR oh-TEHL.

351. Not too expensive.

Não muito caro.

no͞w MOO‿een-toh KAH-roh.

352. I (don't) want to be in the center of town.

(Não) desejo hospedar-me no centro da cidade.

(no͞w) day-ZAY-zhoh ohss-pay-DAHR-may noh SEN-troh dah see-DAH-day.

353. Where it is not noisy.

Onde não há muito barulho.

OHN-day no͞w ah MOO‿een-toh bah-ROOL-yoh.

354. I have a reservation for ——.

Tenho um quarto reservado no ——.

TAY-nyoh o͞o KWAHR-toh ray-sehr-VAH-doh noh ——.

355. I want to make a reservation.

Quero reservar um quarto.

KEH-roh ray-sehr-VAHR o͞o KWAHR-toh.

356. I want a (single, double) room.
Desejo um quarto de (solteiro, casal).
day-ZAY-zhoh ōo KWAHR-toh day (sohl-TAY-roh, kah-ZAHL).

357. (With, without) meals.
(Com, sem) refeições.
(kōh, sāy) ray-fay-SŌYSS.

358. A suite.
Um apartamento.
ōo ah-pahr-tah-MEN-toh.

359. With (bath, shower, twin beds).
Com (banheiro, chuveiro, duas camas de solteiro).
kōh (bah-NYAY-roh, shoo-VAY-roh, DOO-ahss KAH-mahss day sohl-TAY-roh).

360. A room with a window.
Um quarto com janela.
ōo KWAHR-toh kōh zhah-NEH-lah.

361. In the front, at the back.
De frente, de fundo.
day FREN-tay, day FOON-doh.

362. For (a few, two) days.
Por (uns, dois) dias.
pohr (ōoz, doyss) DEE-ahss.

363. For tonight.
Por esta noite.
pohr ESS-tah NOY-tay.

364. For —— persons.
Para —— pessôas.
PAH-rah —— peh-SOH-ahss.

365. What is the rate a day?
Qual é a diária?
kwahl eh ah dee-AH-ryah?

366. A week, a month?
Por semana, por mês?
pohr say-MAH-nah, pohr mayss?

367. On what floor?
Em que andar?
ay kay ahn-DAHR?

368. Upstairs, downstairs.
Em cima, em baixo.
ay SEE-mah ay BIE-shoh.

369. Is there an elevator?
Há elevador?
ah eh-leh-vah-DOHR?

370. Running water, hot water.
Água corrente, água quente.
AH-gwah koh-RREN-tay, AH-gwah KEN-tay.

371. I want a room higher up.
Desejo um quarto num andar mais alto.
day-ZAY-zhoh oo KWAHR-toh noo ahn-DAHR MAH_eess AHL-toh.

372. On a lower floor.
Num andar mais baixo.
noo ahn-DAHR MAH_eess BIE-shoh.

373. I should like to see the room.
Gostaria de ver o quarto.
gaws-tah-REE-ah day vehr oh KWAHR-toh.

374. Where is the bathroom?
Onde fica o banheiro?
OHN-day FEE-kah oh bah-NYAY-roh?

375. I (do not) like this one.
(Não) gosto dêste.
(now) GAWS-toh DAYSS-tay.

376. Have you something better?
Tem um melhor?
tah oo mehl-YOHR?

377. Cheaper, larger, smaller.
Mais barato, maior, menor.
MAH eess bah-RAH-toh, mah-YOHR, meh-NOHR.

378. With more (light, air).
Com mais (luz, ar).
koh MAH eess (looss, ahr).

379. I have baggage at the station.
Tenho bagagem na estação.
TAY-nyoh bah-GAH-zhay nah ess-tah-SOW.

380. Send me a bellboy.
Mande-me um mensageiro.
MAHN-day-may oo men-sah-ZHAY-roh.

381. Will you send for my bags?
Quer mandar buscar minhas maletas?
kehr mahn-DAHR boos-KAHR MEE-nyahs mah-LAY-tahss?

382. Here is the check for my trunk.

Aquí está o recibo da minha mala.

ah-KEE ess-TAH oh ray-SEE-boh dah MEE-nyah MAH-lah.

383. Please send —— to my room.

Mande —— para o meu quarto, por favor.

MAHN-day —— PAH-rah oh MAY‿oo KWAHR-toh, pohr fah-VOHR.

384. Ice, a pitcher of ice water.

Gêlo, uma jarra de água gelada.

ZHAY-lo, OO-mah ZHAH-rrah day AH-gwah zhay-LAH-dah.

385. Please call me at —— o'clock.

Chame-me as —— horas, por favor.

SHAH-may-may ahss —— OH-rahss, pohr fah-VOHR.

386. I want breakfast in my room.

Desejo o café no meu quarto.

day-ZAY-zhoh oh kah-FEH noh MAY‿oo KWAHR-toh.

387. Please get me ——.

Traga-me ——, por favor.

TRAH-gah-may ——, pohr fah-VOHR.

388. Could I have some laundry done?

Posso mandar umas roupas para a lavanderia?

PAW-soh mahn-DAHR OO-mahss ROH-pahss PAH-rah ah lah-vahn-day-REE-ah?

389. I want some things pressed.
Desejo algumas roupas passadas.
day-ZAY-zhoh ahl-GOO-mahss ROH-pahss pah-SAH-dahss.

390. My room key, please.
A chave do meu quarto, por favor.
ah SHAH-vay doh MAY⁀oo KWAHR-toh, pohr fah-VOHR.

391. Are there any letters for ——?
Há cartas para ——?
ah KAHR-tahss PAH-rah ——?

392. When does the mail come?
Quando chegam as cartas?
KWAHN-doh SHAY-gow ahss KAHR-tahss?

393. What is my room number?
Qual é o numero do meu quarto?
kwahl eh oh NOO-may-roh doh MAY⁀oo KWAHR-toh?

394. I am leaving at —— o'clock.
Partirei às —— horas.
pahr-tee-RAY ahss —— OH-rahss.

395. We will return at 12:30.
Voltaremos ao meio-dia e meio.
vohl-tah-RAY-mohss ow MAY-yoh-DEE-ah ee MAY-yoh.

396. In an hour, later.
Em uma hora, mais tarde.
ay OO-mah OH-rah, MAH⁀eess TAHR-day.

397. Please make out my bill.

Faça o favor de tirar a minha conta.

*FAH-sah oh fah-VOHR day tee-RAHR ah
MEE-nyah KOHN-tah.*

398. I should like to speak to the manager.

Gostaria de falar com o gerente.

*gaws-tah-REE-ah day fah-LAHR koh oh
zheh-REN-tay.*

399. Can one store baggage here until ——?

Pode-se guardar bagagem aquí até ——?

*PAW-day-say gwahr-DAHR bah-GAH-zhay
ah-KEE ah-TEH——?*

400. Please forward my mail to ——.

Reenvie minha correspondência para
——, por favor.

*ray-en-VEE-ay MEE-nyah koh-rayss-pohn-
DEN-syah PAH-rah——, pohr fah-VOHR.*

CHAMBERMAID
A ARRUMADEIRA

402. Do not disturb me early.

Não me incomode cêdo.

now may een-koh-MOH-day SAY-doh.

403. Please change the sheets today.

Faça o favor de mudar os lençóis hoje.

*FAH-sah oh fah-VOHR day moo-DAHR ohss
len-SOYSS OH-zhay.*

404. Bring me another pillow.
Traga-me outro travesseiro.
TRAH-gah-may OH-troh trah-vay-SAY-roh.

405. A pillow case, a bath mat.
Uma fronha, um tapête de banho.
OO-mah FROH-nyah, $\overline{oo}$ tah-PAY-tay day BAH-nyoh.

406. More hangers, a glass.
Mais cabides, um copo.
MAH⏜eess kah-BEE-dayss, $\overline{oo}$ KAW-poh.

407. Soap, towels, a candle.
Sabonete, toalhas, uma vela.
sah-boh-NAY-tay, TWAHL-yahss, OO-mah VEH-lah.

408. Drinking water, toilet paper.
Água para beber, papel higiênico.
AH-gwah PAH-rah bay-BEHR, pah-PEHL ee-zhee-AY-nee-koh.

409. Is there always hot water?
Há sempre água quente?
ah SEM-pray AH-gwah KEN-tay?

410. Please spray for mosquitoes.
Faça o favor de vaporizar flit para os mosquitos.
FAH-sah oh fah-VOHR day vah-poh-ree-ZAHR fleet PAH-rah ohss mohss-KEE-tohss.

411. Please come back later.
Faça o favor de voltar mais tarde.
FAH-sah oh fah-VOHR day vohl-TAHR MAH⏜eess TAHR-day.

APARTMENT
O APARTAMENTO

413. I want a furnished apartment.
Desejo um apartamento mobilado.
day-ZAY-zhoh oo ah-pahr-tah-MEN-toh moh-bee-LAH-doh.

414. I want a living room, —— bedrooms.
Desejo uma sala de visitas, —— dormitórios.
day-ZAY-zhoh OO-mah SAH-lah day vee-ZEE-tahss, —— dohr-mee-TAW-ryohss.

415. A dining room, a kitchen.
Uma sala de jantar, uma cozinha.
OO-mah SAH-lah day zhahn-TAHR, OO-mah koh-ZEE-nyah.

416. A private bath.
Um banheiro privativo.
oo bah-NYAY-roh pree-vah-TEE-voh.

417. Is the linen furnished?
Fornecem lencóis?
fohr-NEH-say len-SOYSS?

418. How much is it a month?
Quanto é por mês?
KWAHN-toh eh pohr mayss?

419. The blankets, silver and dishes.
Os cobertores, os talheres e pratos.
ohss koh-behr-TOH-rayss, tahl-YEH-rayss ee PRAH-tohss.

420. Can I get a maid?

Posso arranjar uma empregada?

PAW-soh ah-rrahn-ZHAR OO-mah em-pray-GAH-dah?

421. Do you know a good cook?

Conhece uma bôa cozinheira?

kohn-NYEH-say OO-mah BOH-ah koh-zee-NYAY-rah?

422. Where can I rent a garage?

Onde posso alugar uma garage?

OHN-day PAW-soh ah-loo-GAHR OO-mah gah-RAH-zhay?

RESTAURANT AND FOOD
RESTAURANTE E COMIDA

Restaurant   O restaurante

424. Where is there a good restaurant?

Onde fica um bom restaurante?

OHN-day FEE-kah oo boh ress-tow-RAHN-tay?

425. For breakfast, for lunch.

Para café, para almôço.

PAH-rah kah-FEH, PAH-rah ahl-MOH-soh.

426. Dinner, a sandwich.

Jantar, um sanduiche.

zhahn-TAHR, oo sahn-DWEE-shay.

427. Between what hours is dinner served?

Entre que horas servem o jantar?

EN-tray kay OH-rahss SEHR-vay oh zhahn-TAHR?

428. Can we (lunch, dine) now?

Podemos (almoçar, jantar) agora?

poh-DAY-mohss (ahl-moh-SAHR, zhahn-TAHR) ah-GOH-rah?

429. There are two (five) of us.

Somos dois (cinco).

SOH-mohss doyss (SEEN-koh).

430. The head waiter, the waitress.

O chefe dos garçons, a garçonete.

oh SHEH-fay dohss gahr-SOHSS, ah gahr-soh-NEH-tay.

431. Waiter!

Garçon!

gahr-SOH!

432. Give me a table near the window.

Dê-me uma mesa perto da janela.

DAY-may OO-mah MAY-zah PEHR-toh dah zhah-NEH-lah.

433. At the side, in the corner.

Ao lado, no canto.

ow LAH-doh, noh KAHN-toh.

434. Is this table reserved?

Esta mesa está reservada?

ESS-tah MAY-zah ess-TAH ray-zehr-VAH-dah?

435. We want to dine à la carte.

Desejamos um jantar do menú.

day-zay-ZHAH-mohss oo zhan-TAHR doh may-NOO.

436. Please serve us quickly.
Faça o favor de servir-nos depressa.
FAH-sah oh fah-VOHR day sehr-VEER-nohss day-PREH-sah.

437. Bring me the menu.
Traga-me o menú.
TRAH-gah-may oh may-NOO.

438. The wine list.
A lista de vinhos.
ah LEE-stah day VEE-nyohss.

439. I want something simple.
Desejo qualquer coisa simples.
day-ZAY-zhoh kwahl-KEHR KOY-sah SEEM-playss.

440. Not too peppery.
Não tão apimentado.
now tow ah-pee-men-TAH-doh.

441. A napkin, a glass.
Um guardanapo, um copo.
oo gwahr-dah-NAH-poh oo KAW-poh.

442. A plate, a knife.
Um prato, uma faca.
oo PRAH-toh, OO-mah FAH-kah.

443. A fork, a large spoon.
Um garfo, uma colher grande.
oo GAHR-foh, OO-mah kohl-YEHR GRAHN-day.

444. A teaspoon.
Uma colher de chá.
OO-mah kohl-YEHR day SHAH.

445. The bread, the butter.
O pão, a manteiga.
oh pow, ah mahn-TAY-gah.

446. The milk, the sugar.
O leite, o açucar.
oh LAY-tay, oh ah-SOO-kahr.

447. The salt, the pepper.
O sal, a pimenta.
oh sahl, ah pee-MEHN-tah.

448. The sauce, the vinegar.
O môlho, o vinagre.
oh MOHL-yoh, oh vee-NAH-gray.

449. The oil.   (Salad oil.)
O azeite.
oh ah-ZAY-tay.

450. This is not clean.
Isto não está limpo.
EESS-toh now ess-TAH LEEM-poh.

451. It is dirty.
Está sujo.
ess-TAH SOO-zhoh.

452. A little more of this.
Um pouco mais disto.
oo POH-koh MAH eess DEES-toh.

453. I have had enough, thanks.
Estou satisfeito, obrigado.
ess-TOH sah-teess-FAY-toh oh-bree-GAH-doh.

454. I like it rare (well done).
Eu gosto sangrento (bem passado).
EH‿oo GAWS-toh (sahn-GREN-toh, ba̅y pah-SAH-doh).

455. This is overcooked.
Isto está cozido demais.
EESS-toh koh-ZEE-doh day-MAY‿eess.

456. This is not cooked enough.
Isto não está bastante cozido.
EESS-toh no̅w ess-TAH bahss-TAHN-tay koh-ZEE-doh.

457. This is too (tough, sweet, sour).
Isto está (duro, dôce, azêdo).
EESS-toh ess-TAH (DOO-roh, DOH-say, ah-ZAY-doh).

458. This is cold.
Isto está frio.
EESS-toh ess-TAH FREE-oh.

459. Take it away.
Leve-o.
LEH-vay-oh.

460. I did not order this.
Eu não pedí isto.
EH‿oo no̅w pay-DEE EESS-toh.

461. May I change this for (fruit)?
Posso trocar isto por (fruta)?
PAW-soh troh-KAHR EESS-toh pohr (FROO-tah)?

462. Ask the headwaiter to come here.
Peça ao chefe dos garçons para vir aquí.
PEH-sah ow SHEH-fay dohss gahr-SŌHSS PAH-rah veer ah-KEE.

463. The check, please.
A conta, por favor.
ah KOHN-tah, pohr fah-VOHR.

464. Kindly pay at the cashier's.
Faça o favor de pagar na caixa.
FAH-sah oh fah-VOHR day pah-GAHR nah KIE-shah.

465. Is the tip included?
A gorjeta está incluída?
ah gohr-ZHAY-tah ess-TAH een-kloo-EE-dah?

466. Is there a service charge?
Cobram o serviço?
KOH-brow oh sehr-VEE-soh?

467. Keep the change for yourself.
Pode ficar com o trôco.
PAW-day fee-KAHR kōh oh TROH-koh.

468. There is a mistake in the bill.
Há um engano na conta.
ah ōo en-GAH-noh nah KOHN-tah.

469. What are these charges for?
Estas contas a que correspondem?
ESS-tahss KOHN-tahss ah kay koh-rrayss-POHN-day?

CAFÉ or BAR
O BAR

472. The bartender. O botiquineiro.
oh boh-tay-kee-NAY-roh.

473. The waiter. O garçon. *oh gahr-SOH.*

474. A cocktail. Um coquetél.
oo koh-kay-TEHL.

475. A fruit drink. Um refrêsco.
oo ray-FRAYSS-koh.

476. A highball. Um uisque com soda.
oo WEESS-kay koh SOH-dah.

477. Ice water. Água gelada.
AH-gwah zheh-LAH-dah.

478. A liqueur. Um licôr. *oo lee-KOHR.*

479. Brandy. Aguardente *or* conhaque.
ah-gwahr-DEN-tay or koh-NYAH-kay.

480. (Light, dark) beer.
Cerveja (clara, escura).
sehr-VAY-zhah (KLAH-rah, ess-KOO-rah).

481. (Sweet, dry) wine. Vinho (dôce, sêco).
VEE-nyoh (DOH-say, SAY-koh).

482. (White, red) wine.
Vinho (branco, tinto).
VEE-nyoh (BRAHN-koh, TEEN-toh).

483. A soft drink (orange, pineapple grape).
Um refrêsco (de laranja, de abacaxí, de uva).
oo ray-FRAYSS-koh (day lah-RAHN-zhah, day ah-bah-kah-SHEE, day OO-vah).

484. A bottle, a glass of ——.
Uma garafa, um copo de ——.
OO-mah gah-RRAH-fah, oo KAW-poh day ——.

485. Let's have another. Vamos repetir.
VAH-mohss ray-pay-TEER.

FOOD AND DRINK

This section has been alphabetized in Portuguese to facilitate the tourist's reading of menus in Portuguese.

488. Abacaxí. *ah-bah-kah-SHEE.*
Pineapple.

489. Abóbora. *ah-BAW-boh-rah.* **Squash.**

490. Agua mineral. *AH-gwah mee-nay-RAHL.*
Mineral water.

491. Aipo. *IE-poh.* **Celery.**

492. Alface. *ahl-FAH-say.* **Lettuce.**

493. Alho. *AHL-yoh.* **Garlic.**

494. Ameixas. *ah-MAY-shahss.* **Prunes.**

495. Amêndoas. *ah-MEN-doh-ahss.*
Almonds.

496. Amendoim. *ah-men-doh-$\overline{EE}$.* **Peanuts.**

497. Amóras. *ah-MAW-rahss.* **Berries.**

498. Almôndegas. *AHL-MOHN-day-gahss.*
Meat balls.

499. Anchovas. *ahn-SHOH-vahss.* **Anchovy.**

500. Assado. *ah-SAH-doh.* **Roast.**

501. Arrôs. *ah-ROHSS.* **Rice.**

502. Avêia. *ah-VAY-yah.* **Oatmeal.**

503. Azeitonas. *ah-ZAY-toh-nahss.* **Olives.**

504. Bacalhau. *bah-kahl-YOW.* **Cod fish.**

505. Bacon. *bah-K$\overline{OH}$.* **Bacon.**

506. Batatas (doces). *bah-TAH-tahss.*
(Sweet) potatoes.

507. Beringela. *bay-reen-ZHEH-lah.*
Eggplant.

508. Bife. *BEE-fay.* **Beefsteak.**

509. Biscoitos. *bees-KOY-tohss.* **Cookies.**

510. Bolacha. *boh-LAH-shah.* **Crackers.**

511. Bôlo. *BOH-loh.* **Cake.**

512. Bombons. *bohm-B$\overline{OH}$SS.* **Candy.**

513. Café. *kah-FEH.* **Coffee.**

514. Uma média. *OO-mah MEH-dyah.*
Coffee with milk.

515. Cafézinho. *kah-feh-ZEE-nyoh.*
Small cup of black coffee.

516. Camarão. *kah-mah-ROW.* **Shrimp.**

517. Carangueijo. *kah-rahn-GAY-zhoh.*
Crab.

518. Carne. *KAHR-nay.* **Meat.**

519. Carneiro. *kahr-NAY-roh.* **Mutton.**

520. Castanhas. *kahss-TAH-nyahss.* **Nuts.**

521. Cebola. *say-BOH-lah.* **Onion.**

522. Cenouras. *seh-NOH-rahss.* **Carrots.**

523. Cerejas. *say-RAY-zhahss.* **Cherries.**

524. Chá. *shah.* **Tea.**

525. Champanhe. *sham-PAH-nyay.*
Champagne.

526. Chouriço. *shoh-REE-soh.* **Sausage.**

527. Churrasco. *shoo-RRAHSS-koh.*
Barbecue.

528. Coêlho. *koh-AYL-yoh.* **Rabbit.**

529. Cogumelos. *koh-goo-MEH-lohss.*
Mushrooms.

530. Costelêta de porco.
koh-stay-LAY-tah day POHR-koh.
Pork chop.

531. Couveflor. *koh-vay-FLOHR.*
Cauliflower.

532. Crême. *KREH-may.* **Cream.**

533. Damascos.   *dah-MAHSS-kohss.*
Apricots.

534. Empada.   *em-PAH-dah.*   **Meat pie.**

535. Ervilhas.   *ehr-VEEL-yahss.*   **Peas.**

536. Espargos.   *ess-PAHR-gohss.*   **Asparagus.**

537. Espinafre.   *ess-pee-NAH-fray.*
Spinach.

538. Fatia.   *fah-TEE-ah.*   **Slice.**

539. Fatias frias.   *fah-TEE-ahss FREE-ahss.*
Cold cuts.

540. Feijão.   *fay-ZHOW.*   **Beans.**

541. Feijão de vagens.
fay-ZHOW day VAH-zhayz.
Green beans.

542. Feijoada.   *fay-zhoh-AH-dah.*
**Black beans stewed with dried meat,
bacon, sausage, etc.**

543. Fígado.   *FEE-gah-doh.*   **Liver.**

544. Figos.   *FEE-gohss.*   **Figs.**

545. Filé (mignon).   *fee-LEH (mee-NYOH).*
Tenderloin steak.

546. Galinha (assada).
gah-LEE-nyah (ah-SAH-dah).
(Roast) chicken.

547. Geléa.   *zheh-LAY-ah.*   **Jelly.**

548. Gêlo.   *ZHAY-loh.*   **Ice.**

549. Guisado. *ghee-ZAH-doh.* **Stew.**

550. Lagôsta. *lah-GOHSS-tah.* **Lobster.**

551. Laranja. *lah-RAHN-zhah.* **Orange.**

552. Laranjada. *lah-rahn-ZHAH-dah.*
Orangeade.

553. Legumes. *lay-GOO-mayss.* **Vegetables.**

554. Leite. *LAY-tay.* **Milk.**

555. Limão. *lee-MOW.* **Lemon.**

556. Limonada. *lee-moh-NAH-dah.*
Lemonade.

557. Lingua. *LEEN-gwah.* **Tongue.**

558. Lombo (de vitela).
LOHM-boh (day vee-TEH-lah).
(**Veal**) **loin.**

559. Maçã. *mah-SAH.* **Apple.**

560. Macarrão. *mah-kah-RROW.*
Macaroni.

561. Mamão. *mah-MOW.* **Papaya.**

562. Manteiga. *mahn-TAY-gah.* **Butter.**

563. Melancia. *meh-lahn-SEE-ah.*
Watermelon.

564. Milho. *MEEL-yoh.* **Corn.**

565. Morangos. *moh-RAHN-gohss.*
Strawberries.

566. Mortadela. *mohr-tah-DEH-lah.*
Bologna.

567. Mostarda. *mohss-TAHR-dah.*
Mustard.

568. Nabos. *NAH-bohss.* **Turnips.**

569. Ovos (cozidos, quentes, pochê).
AW-vohss (koh-ZEE-dohss, KEN-tayss, poh-SHAY).
Eggs (hard-boiled, soft-boiled, poached).

570. Ovos (estrelados, mexidos).
AW-vohss (ess-tray-LAH-dohss, meh-SHEE-dohss).
Eggs (fried, scrambled).

571. Pãezinhos. *pie-ZEE-nyohss.* **Rolls.**

572. Pão. *pow.* **Bread.**

573. Passas. *PAH-sahss.* **Raisins.**

574. Pato. *PAH-toh.* **Duck.**

575. Peixe (frito, assado).
PAY-shay (FREE-toh, ah-SAH-doh).
(Fried, baked) fish.

576. Pêra. *PAY-rah.* **Pear.**

577. Perna de carneiro.
PEHR-nah day kahr-NAY-roh.
Leg of lamb.

578. Perú. *pay-ROO.* **Turkey.**

579. Pêssego. *PAY-say-goh.* **Peach.**

580. Picadinho. *pee-kah-DEE-nyoh.*
Chopped meat.

581. Pimenta do reino.
pee-MEN-tah doh RAY-noh.
Black pepper.

582. Pôrco. *POHR-koh.* **Pork.**

583. Presunto. *pray-ZOON-toh.* **Ham.**

584. Pudim. *poo-DEE.* **Pudding.**

585. Puré de batatas.
poo-RAY day bah-TAH-tahss.
Mashed potatoes.

586. Queijo. *KAY-zhoh.* **Cheese.**

587. Rabanete. *rah-bah-NAY-tay.* **Radish.**

588. Recheio. *ray-SHAY-yoh.* **Stuffing.**

589. Repôlho. *ray-POHL-yoh.* **Cabbage.**

590. Rins. *reess.* **Kidney.**

591. Rosbife. *rohz-BEE-fay.* **Roast beef.**

592. Sal. *sahl.* **Salt.**

593. Môlho. *MOHL-yoh.* **Sauce.**

594. Salsicha. *sahl-SEE-shah.* **Sausage.**

595. Sôpa. *SOH-pah.* **Soup.**

596. Sorvête. *sohr-VAY-tay.* **Ice cream.**

597. Tâmaras. *TAH-mah-rahss.* **Dates.**

598. Tomate. *toh-MAH-tay.* **Tomato.**

599. Torrada. *toh-RRAH-dah.* **Toast.**

600. Touchinho. *toh-SEE-nyoh.*
Smoked slab baçon.

601. Uvas. *OO-vahss.* **Grapes.**

602. Verduras. *vehr-DOO-rahss.*
Green leafy vegetables.

603. Vinagre. *vee-NAH-gray.* **Vinegar.**

604. Vitela. *vee-TEH-lah.* **Veal.**

CHURCH AND RECREATION
A IGREJA E A RECREAÇÃO

Church. A igreja

606. Where is the nearest Catholic church?
Onde fica a igreja católica mais próxima
daquí?
*OHN-day FEE-kah ah ee-GRAY-zhah kah-
TAW-lee-kah MAH‿eess PRAWS-see-
mah dah-KEE?*

607. We wish to attend an Anglican service.
Desejamos assistir a um culto anglicano.
*day-zah-ZHAH-mohss ah-seess-TEER ah ōō
KOOL-toh ahn-glee-KAH-noh.*

608. Is there a synagogue?
Há uma sinagoga?
ah OO-mah see-nah-GAW-gah?

**609. Where is there a church service in
English?**
Onde há um culto em inglês?
OHN-day ah ōō KOOL-toh ay̆ een-GLAYSS?

610. For Baptists, for Methodists.
Para Batistas, para Metodistas.
PAH-rah bah-TEES-tahss, PAH-rah meh-toh-DEESS-tahss.

611. For Presbyterians.
Para Presbiterianos.
PAH-rah prehsss-bee-teh-ree-AH-nohss.

612. When is (the service, the mass)?
Onde é (o culto, a missa)?
OHN-day eh (oh KOOL-toh, ah MEE-sah)?

613. Can we go to communion?
Podemos comungar?
poh-DAY-mohss koh-MOON-gahr?

614. Is there an English-speaking priest?
Há um padre que fale inglês?
ah ōō PAH-dray kay FAH-lay een-GLAYSS?

SIGHTSEEING
VISITAS A LUGARES DE INTERESSE

616. I want a guide who speaks English.
Desejo um guía que fale inglês.
day-ZAY-zhoh ōō GHEE-ah kay FAH-lay een-GLAYSS.

617. What do you charge (per hour, per day)?
Quanto cobra (por hora, por dia)?
KWAHN-toh KAW-brah (pohr OH-rah, pohr DEE-ah)?

618. I am interested in archeology.
  Estou interessado em arqueologia.
  ess-TOH en-teh-ray-SAH-doh ay ahr-kay-oh-loh-ZHEE-ah.

619. Native arts and crafts.
  Objetos de artes nativas.
  awb-ZHEH-tohss day AHR-tayss nah-TEE-vahss.

620. Painting, ruins.
  Pintura, ruínas.
  peen-TOO-rah, roo-EE-nahss.

621. Sculpture.
  Escultura.
  ess-KOOL-too-rah.

622. The cathedral.
  A catedral.
  ah kah-tay-DRAHL.

623. The lake, the library.
  O lago, a biblioteca.
  oh LAH-goh, ah bee-blyoh-TAY-kah.

624. The market, the monastery.
  O mercado, o mosteiro.
  oh MEHR-kah-doh, oh mohss-TAY-roh.

625. The mountain, the park.
  A montanha, o parque.
  ah mohn-TAH-nyah, oh PAHR-kay.

626. The palace, the promenade.
  O palácio, o passeio.
  oh pah-LAH-syoh, oh pah-SAY-yoh.

627. I shall have time to visit the museums.

Terei tempo de visitar os museus.

tay-RAY TEM-poh day vee-zee-TAHR ohss moo-ZAY͜ooss.

628. Is it open (still)?

(Ainda) está aberto?

(ah-EEN-dah) ess-TAH ah-BEHR-toh?

629. How long does it stay open?

Até que hora fica aberta?

ah-TAY kay OH-rah FEE-kah ah-BEHR-tah?

630. How long must we wait?

Quanto tempo temos que esperar?

KWAHN-toh TEM-poh TAY-mohss kay ess-peh-RAHR?

631. Where is the entrance (exit)?

Onde fica a entrada (a saida)?

OHN-day FEE-cah ah (en-TRAH-dah, ah sah-EE-dah)?

632. What is the entrance fee?

Quanto se paga para entrar?

KWAHN-toh say PAH-gah PAH-rah en-TRAHR?

633. Do we need a guide?

Precisamos de um guía?

pray-see-ZAH-mohss day ōo GHEE-ah?

634. How much is (the catalog, guide book)?

Quanto custa (o catálogo, o guia)?

KWAHN-toh KOOSS-tah (oh kah-TAH-loh-goh, oh GHEE-ah)?

635. May I take photographs?

Posso tirar fotografias?

PAW-soh tee-RAHR foh-toh-grah-FEE-ahss?

636. Do you sell (post-cards, souvenirs)?

Vende (postais, lembranças)?

VEN-day (pohss-TAH‿ees, lem-BRAHN-sahss)?

637. Have you a book in English about ——?

Tem um livro em inglês sobre ——?

tay̅ o̅o LEE-vroh ay̅ een-GLAYSS SOH-bray ——?

638. Take me back to the hotel now.

Leve-me ao hotel agora.

LEH-vay-may ow oh-TEHL ah-GOH-rah.

639. Go back by way of ——.

Volte por ——.

VOHL-tay pohr ——.

AMUSEMENTS
OS DIVERTIMENTOS

641. What is there to do today?

O que há para fazer hoje?

oh kay ah PAH-rah fah-ZEHR OH-zhay?

642. A concert, a festival, a football game.
  Um concêrto, um festival, um jôgo de
    futeból.
  o͞o kohn-SEHR-toh, o͞o fehss-tee-VAHL, o͞o
    ZHOH-goh day foo-tay-BAWL.

643. Horse races, dances, movies.
  Corridas de cavalos, bailes, cinemas.
  koh-REE-dahss day kah-VAH-lohss, BIE-
    layss, see-NAY-mahss.

644. The beach, tennis, golf.
  A praia, o tenis, o golf.
  ah PRAH-yah, oh TAY-neess, oh GOHL-fay.

645. A night club, the opera, the theater.
  Uma boite, a ópera, o teatro.
  OO-mah BWAH-tay, ah AW-pay-rah, oh
    tay-AH-troh.

646. Is there a matinée today?
  Há matinée hoje?
  ah mah-tee-NAY OH-zhay?

647. When does the performance start?
  A que hora começa?
  ah kay OH-rah koh-MEH-sah?

648. The floor show is at about ten.
  O show começa mais ou menos às dez.
  oh shoh koh-MEH-sah MAH͜eess oh MEH-
    nohss ahss dehss.

649. The cover charge, the minimum.
O serviço, o mínimo.
oh sehr-VEE-soh, oh MEE-nee-moh.

650. Where can we go to dance?
Onde podemos dansar?
OHN-day poh-DAY-mohss dahn-SAHR?

651. What should I wear?
Que devo usar?
kay DAY-voh oo-ZAHR?

652. Have you any seats for tonight?
Tem cadeiras para esta noite?
tay kah-DAY-rahss PAH-rah ESS-tah NOY-tay?

653. An orchestra seat, reserved seat.
Um lugar na platéia, um assento reservado.
oo loo-GAHR nah PLAH-tay-yah, oo ah-SEN-toh ray-sehr-VAH-doh.

654. In the balcony, a box.
No balcão, uma friza.
noh bahl-KOW, OO-mah FREE-zah.

655. The checkroom, the usher.
O guarda-roupa, o vagalume.
oh gwahr-dah-ROH-pah, oh vah-gah-LOO-may.

656. Can I (see, hear) well from there?
Posso (ver, ouvir) bem de lá?
PAW-soh (vehr, oo-VEER) bay day lah?

657. Not very near, (far).

Não muito perto, (longe).

$\overline{now}$ *MOO‿een-toh PEHR-toh, (LOHN-zhay).*

658. (The music, the orchestra) is excellent.

(A música, a orquestra) é excelente.

(*ah MOO-zee-kah ah ohr-KEHSS-trah) eh ayss-say-LEN-tay.*

659. This is very entertaining (funny).

Isto é muito divertido.

EESS-toh eh MOO‿een-toh dee-vehr-TEE-doh.

660. May I have this dance?

Quer dar-me o prazer desta dança?

kehr DAHR-may oh prah-ZEHR DESS-tah DAHN-sah?

SHOPPING AND PERSONAL SERVICES
COMPRAS E SERVIÇOS PESSOAIS

Shopping.   Compras.

661. I want to go shopping.

Desejo fazer compras.

day-ZAY-zhoh fah-ZEHR KOHM-prahss.

662. Where is there a bakery?

Onde há uma padaria?

OHN-day ah OO-mah pah-dah-REE-ah?

663. A candy store, a cigar store.
Uma bombonière, uma tabacaria.
OO-mah bohm-boh-NYEHR, OO-mah tah-bah-kah-REE-ah.

664. A clothing store, a department store.
Uma loja de roupas feitas, uma loja de artigos gerais.
OO-mah LAW-zhah day ROH-pahss FAY-tahss, OO-mah LAW-zhah day ahr-TEE-gohss geh-RAH͜ees.

665. A drug store, a grocery.
Uma drogaria, uma mercearia.
OO-mah draw-gah-REE-ah, OO-mah mehr-say-ah-REE-ah.

666. A hat shop, a jewelry store.
Uma chapelaria, uma joalheria.
OO-mah shah-peh-lah-REE-ah, OO-mah zhoh-ahl-yay-REE-ah.

667. A hardware store.
Uma casa de ferragens.
OO-mah KAH-sah day fay-RAH-gāyss.

668. A market, a shoe store.
Um mercado, uma sapataria.
ōō mehr-KAH-doh, OO-mah sah-pah-tah-REE-ah.

669. A tailor shop.
Uma alfaiataria.
OO-mah ahl-fah-yah-tah-REE-ah.

670. (Shoe, watch) repairs.
Consêrtos de (sapatos, relógios).
kohn-SEHR-tohss day (sah-PAH-tohss, ray-LAW-zhohss).

671. Sale; bargain sale.
Venda; liquidação.
VEN-dah; lee-kee-dah-SOW.

672. I want to buy ——.
Desejo comprar ——.
day-ZAY-zhoh kohm-PRAHR ——.

673. I (do not) like this.
(Não) gosto disto.
(now) GAW-stoh DEES-toh.

674. How much is that?
Quanto custa isso?
KWAHN-toh KOOS-tah EE-soh?

675. I prefer something (better, cheaper).
Prefiro algo (melhor, mais barato).
pray-FEE-roh AHL-goh (mehl-YOHR, MAH_eess bah-RAH-toh).

676. Show me some others.
Mostre-me outros.
MAWSS-tray-may OH-trohss.

677. Please show me some samples.
Mostre-me algumas amostras, por favor.
MAWS-tray-may ahl-GOO-mahss ah-MAWSS-trahss, pohr fah-VOHR.

678. May I try this on?
Posso experimentar êste?
PAW-soh ess-peh-ree-men-TAHR AYSS-tay?

679. Can I order one?
Posso mandar fazer um?
PAW-soh mahn-DAHR fah-ZEHR o͞o?

680. How long will it take?
Quanto tempo levará?
KWAHN-toh TEM-poh leh-vah-RAH?

681. Please take my measurements.
Faça o favôr de tirar minhas medidas.
FAH-sah oh fah-VOHR day tee-RAHR MEE-nyahss may-DEE-dahss.

See also MEASUREMENTS, p. 115.

682. It does not fit.
Não cae bem.
no͞w kie ba͞y.

683. It is too (large, small).
É muito (grande, pequeno).
eh MOO‿een-toh (GRAHN-day, pay-KAY-noh).

684. It is not becoming.
Não vai bem.
no͞w vie ba͞y.

685. Will you wrap this please?
Quer embrulhar isto, por favor?
kehr em-brool-YAHR EESS-toh, pohr fah-VOHR?

686. Pack this for shipment to ——.
Empacote isto para embarcar para ——.
em-pah-KAW-tay EESS-toh PAH-rah em-bahr-KAHR PAH-rah ——.

687. Whom do I pay?
A quem devo pagar?
ah kay DAY-voh pah-GAHR?

POST OFFICE
O CORRÊIO

689. Where is the post office?
Onde fica o Corrêio?
OHN-day FEE-kah oh koh-RRAY-yoh?

690. (A post card, a letter) to ——.
(Um cartão postal, uma carta) para ——.
oo kahr-TOW pawss-TAHL, OO-mah KAHR-tah) PAH-rah ——.

691. How many stamps do I need?
De quantos sêlos preciso?
day KWAHN-tohss SAY-lohss pray-SEE-zoh?

692. I want five stamps of sixty centavos.
Quero cinco sêlos de sessenta centavos.
KEH-roh SEEN-koh SAY-lohss day say-SEN-tah sen-TAH-vohss.

693. There is nothing dutiable in this.
Não há nada sujeito a impôsto nisto.
now ah NAH-dah soo-ZHAY-toh ah eem-POHSS-toh NEESS-toh.

694. Will this go out today?
Isto sairá hoje?
EESS-toh SAH͜ee-RAH OH-zhay?

695. Give me a receipt, please.
Dê-me um recibo, por favor.
DAY-may o͞o ray-SEE-boh, pohr fah-VOHR.

696. I want to send a money order.
Quero mandar uma ordem postal.
KEH-roh mahn-DAHR OO-mah OHR-da͞y powss-TAHL.

697. To which window do I go?
A que guichê devo ir?
ah kay ghee-ZHAY DAY-voh eer?

698. By air mail, by parcel post.
Via aérea.   Via marítima.
VEE-ah ah-EH-ray-ah.   VEE-ah mah-REE-tee-mah.

699. Registered, special delivery.
Registrada, expressa.
ray-zheess-TRAH-dah, ayss-PREH-sah.

700. Insured.
Segurado.
say-goo-RAH-doh.

BANK
O BANCO

702. Where is the nearest bank?
Onde fica o banco mais próximo?
OHN-day FEE-kah oh BAHN-koh MAH͜eess PRAWSS-see-moh?

703. At which window do I cash this?

Em que guichê posso descontar isto?

ay kay ghee-ZHAY PAW-soh dayss-kohn-TAHR EESS-toh?

704. Can you change this for me?

Pode trocar isto para mim?

PAW-day troh-KAHR EESS-toh PAH-rah mee?

705. Can you cash a check?

Pode descontar um cheque?

PAW-day dayss-kohn-TAHR oo SHEH-kay?

706. Please (do not) give me large bills.

Faça o favor de (não) dar-me notas grandes.

FAH-sah oh fah-VOHR day (now) DAHR-may NAW-tahss GRAHN-dayss.

707. May I have small change?

Pode dar-me trôco miúdo?

PAW-day DAHR-may TROH-koh mee-OO-doh?

708. I have a letter of credit.

Tenho uma carta de crédito.

TAY-nyoh OO-mah KAHR-tah day KREH-dee-toh.

709. Travelers' checks, a draft.

Cheques para viajantes, uma ordem de pagamento.

SHEH-kayss PAH-rah vyah-ZHAHN-tayss, OO-mah OHR-day day pah-gah-MEN-toh.

710. What is the exchange rate on the dollar?

A como está o câmbio do dolar?

ah KOH-moh ess-TAH oh KAHM-byoh doh DAW-lahr?

BOOKSTORE AND STATIONER'S
A LIVRARIA E A PAPELARIA

712. Where is there a bookstore?

Onde há uma livraria?

OHN-day ah OO-mah lee-vrah-REE-ah?

713. A stationer's, a news stand.

Uma papelaria, uma banca de jornais.

OO-mah pah-peh-lah-REE-ah, OO-mah BAHN-kah day zhohr-NAH‿eess.

714. Newspapers, magazines.

Jornais, revistas.

zhor-NAH‿eess, ray-VEESS-tahss.

715. A dictionary, a guide book.

Um dicionário, um guia.

oo dee-syoh-NAH-ryoh, oo GHEE-ah.

716. A map of, a regional map.

Um mapa de, um mapa regional.

oo MAH-pah day, oo MAH-pah ray-zhyoh-NAHL.

717. Playing cards, post cards.

Baralhos, postais.

bah-RAHL-yohss, pawss-TAH‿eess.

718. Greeting cards.
Cartões de cumprimentos.
kahr-TOYSS day koom-pree-MEN-tohss.

719. Writing paper, ink.
Papel para cartas, tinta.
pah-PEHL PAH-rah KAHR-tahss, TEEN-tah.

720. Envelopes (for air mail), a pencil.
Envelopes (aéreos), um lápis.
en-vay-LAW-payss (ah-AY-ray-ohss), oo LAH-peess.

721. A fountain pen, artist's materials.
Uma caneta tinteiro, materiais de pintores.
OO-mah kah-NEH-tah teen-TAY-roh, mah-teh-ree-AH_eess day peen-TOH-rayss.

722. (Strong) string, an eraser.
Corda (forte), uma borracha.
KAWR-dah (FAWR-tay), OO-mah boh-RRAH-shah.

723. Typewriter ribbon.
Fita para máquina de escrever.
FEE-tah PAH-rah MAH-kee-nah day ess-kreh-VEHR.

724. Carbon paper.
Papel carbono.
pah-PEHL kahr-BOH-noh.

725. Tissue paper, wrapping paper.
Papel de sêda, papel de embrulho.
pah-PEHL day SAY-dah, pah-PEHL day em-BROOL-yoh.

CIGAR STORE
CHARUTARIA

727. Where is the nearest cigar store?
Onde fica a charutaria mais próxima?
*OHN-day FEE-kah ah shah-roo-tah-REE-ah
MAH⌣eess PRAWS-see-mah?*

728. I want some cigars.
Quero charutos.
KEH-roh shah-ROO-tohss.

729. A pack of cigarettes, please.
Um maço de cigarros, por favor.
*oo̅ MAH-soh day see-GAH-rohss, pohr fah-
VOHR.*

730. I need a lighter.
Preciso de um isqueiro.
pray-SEE-zoh day oo̅ eess-KAY-roh.

731. Flint, fluid.
Uma pedra de acender, líquido.
*OO-mah PEH-drah day ah-sen-DEHR, LEE-
kee-doh.*

732. Matches, a pipe.
Fósforos, um cachimbo.
FAWSS-foh-rohss, oo̅ kah-SHEEM-boh.

733. Pipe tobacco, a pouch.
Tabaco, uma bôlsa de tobaco.
*tah-BAH-koh, OO-mah BOHL-sah day tah-
BAH-koh.*

BARBER SHOP AND BEAUTY PARLOR
BARBEARIA E SALÃO DE BELEZA

736. Where is there a good barber?
Onde há um bom barbeiro?
OHN-day ah oo boh bahr-BAY-roh?

737. I want a shave.
Quero fazer a barba.
KEH-roh fah-ZEHR ah BAHR-bah.

738. I want a haircut.
Quero cortar o cabêlo.
KEHR-roh kohr-TAHR oh kah-BAY-loh.

739. Not very short.
Não muito curto.
now MOO_een-toh KOOR-toh.

740. Do not cut any off the top.
Não corte nada em cima.
now KOHR-tay NAH-dah ay SEE-mah.

741. At the back and sides.
Atrás e dos lados.
ah-TRAHSS eh dohss LAH-dohss.

742. Do not put on oil.
Não ponha óleo.
now POH-nyah AW-lay-oh.

743. I part my hair on the (other) side.
Parto meu cabêlo do (outro) lado.
PAHR-toh MAY_oo kah-BAY-loh doh (OH-troh) LAH-doh.

744. In the middle.

No meio.

noh MAY-yoh.

745. The water is too (hot, cold).

A agua está muito (quente, fria).

ah AH-gwah ess-TAH MOO‿een-toh (KEN-tay, FREE-ah).

746. I want my shoes shined.

Quero engraxar meus sapatos.

KEH-roh en-grah-SHAR MAY‿ooss sah-PAH-tohss.

747. Can I make an appointment for ——?

Posso marcar uma hora para ——?

PAW-soh mahr-KAHR OO-mah OH-rah PAH-rah ——?

748. I wish a shampoo and set.

Desejo shampú e penteado.

day-ZAY-shoh sham-POO ee pen-tay-AH-doh.

749. A finger wave.

Um penteado a água.

oo pen-tay-AH-doh ah AH-gwah.

750. A permanent wave.

Uma permanente.

OO-mah pehr-mah-NEN-tay.

751. A facial.

Uma massagem.

OO-mah mah-SAH-zhay.

752. A manicure.

Uma manicure.

OO-mah mah-nee-KOO-ray.

PHOTOGRAPHY
A FOTOGRAFIA

754. I want a roll of (color) film.
Quero um rôlo de filme (colorido).
KEH-roh oo ROH-loh day FEEL-may (koh-loh-REE-doh).

755. The size is ——.
O tamanho é ——.
oh tah-MAH-nyoh eh ——.

756. Movie film, for this camera.
Um rôlo de filmar, para esta máquina.
oo ROH-loh day feel-MAHR, PAH-rah ESS-tah MAH-kee-nah.

757. What is the charge for developing a film?
Quanto custa revelar um filme?
KWAHN-to KOOS-tah reh-vay-LAHR oo FEEL-may?

758. For one print of each.
Cada copia.
KAH-dah KAW-pyah.

759. For an enlargement.
Para uma ampliação.
PAH-rah OO-mah ahm-plyah-SOW.

760. My camera is out of order.
Minha máquina está defeituosa.
MEE-nyah MAH-kee-nah ess-TAH day-fay-too-OH-zah.

761. When will they be ready?
Quando estarão prontas?
KWAHN-doh ess-tah-R$\overline{OW}$ PROHN-tahss?

762. Do you rent cameras?
Aluga máquinas?
ahl-LOO-gah MAH-kee-nahss?

763. I should like one for today.
Desejo uma para hoje.
day-ZAY-zhoh OO-mah PAH-rah OH-zhay.

LAUNDRY AND DRY CLEANING
A LAVANDERIA E A TINTURARIA

**765. Where is the nearest (laundry, dry
cleaner)?**
Onde fica a (lavanderia, tintureria) mais
próxima?
*OHN-day FEE-kah ah (lah-vahn-day-REE-
ah,   teen-too-ray-REE-ah)   MAH‿eess
PRAWS-see-mah?*

766. I have something to be washed.
Tenho roupas para lavar.
TAY-nyoh ROH-pahss PAH-rah lah-VAHR.

767. Pressed (brushed, mended).
Passadas, (escovadas, remendadas).
*pah-SAH-dahss (ess-koh-VAH-dahss, reh-men-
DAH-dahss).*

768. For the dry cleaner.
Para a tinturaria.
PAH-rah ah teen-too-rah-REE-ah.

769. Do not wash this in hot water.
Não lave isto em água quente.
no͞o LAH-vay EESS-toh a͞y AH-gwah KEN-tay.

770. Use lukewarm water.
Use água morna.
OO-zay AH-gwah MOHR-nah.

771. Be very careful.
Tenha muito cuidado.
TAY-nyah MOO‿een-toh kwee-DAH-doh.

772. Do not dry this in the sun.
Não ponha isto ao sol.
no͞o POH-nyah EESS-toh ow sawl.

773. Do not starch the collars.
Não engome os colarinhos.
no͞o en-GOH-may ohss kaw-lah-REE-nyohss.

774. When can I have this?
Quando estará pronto?
KWAHN-doh ess-tah-RAH PROHN-toh?

775. Here is the list.
Aquí está o rol.
ah-KEE ess-TAH oh rohl.

776. The belt is missing.
Falta o cinturão.
FAHL-tah oh seen-too-RO͞W.

CLOTHING
AS ROUPAS

779. Apron.   Um avental. $\overline{oo}$ ah-ven-TAHL.

780. Bathing cap.   Uma touca de banho.
OO-mah TOH-kah day BAH-nyoh.

781. Bathing suit.   Um maiô. $\overline{oo}$ mah-YOH.

782. Blouse.   Uma blusa.
OO-mah BLOO-zah.

783. Brassiere.   Um soutien. $\overline{oo}$ soo-TYĀH.

784. Coat.   Um casaco. $\overline{oo}$ kah-ZAH-koh.

785. Collar.   Uma gola.   OO-mah GAW-lah.

786. Diapers.   Fraldas.   FRAHL-dahss.

787. Dress.   Um vestido. $\overline{oo}$ vess-TEE-doh.

788. Garters.   Ligas.   LEE-gahss.

789. Gloves.   Luvas.   LOO-vahss.

790. Handkerchief.   Um lenço.
$\overline{oo}$ LEN-soh.

791. Hat.   Um chapéu. $\overline{oo}$ shah-PEH‿oo.

792. Jacket.   Uma jaquêta.
OO-mah zhah-KAY-tah.

793. Necktie.   Uma gravata.
OO-mah grah-VAH-tah.

794. Nightgown.   Uma camisola.
OO-mah kah-mee-ZOH-lah.

795. Overcoat.   Um sobretudo.
$\overline{oo}$ soh-bray-TOO-doh.

796. Pajamas.   Pijamas.   *pee-ZHAH-mahss.*

797. Panties.   Calças.   *KAHL-sahss.*

798. Petticoat.   Anáguas.   *ah-NAH-gwahss.*

799. Raincoat.   Capa de chuva.
KAH-pah day SHOO-vah.

800. Riding clothes.   Traje de equitação.
TRAH-zhay day ay-kee-tah-SŌW.

801. Robe.   Um robe.   *ōo RAW-bay.*

802. Shirt.   Uma camisa.
OO-mah kah-MEE-zah.

803. Shorts.   Cuécas.   *KWEH-kahss.*

804. Skirt.   Uma sáia.   *OO-mah SAH-yah.*

805. Slip.   Uma combinação.
OO-mah kohm-bee-nah-SŌW.

806. Slippers.   Chinelos.   *shee-NEH-lohss.*

807. Socks.   Meias de homem.
MAY-yahss day OH-māy.

808. (Nylon) stockings.
Meias (nylon) de mulher.
MAY-yahss (NIE-lōh) day mool-YEHR.

809. Suit.   Um terno.   *ōo TEHR-noh.*

810. Suspenders.   Suspensórios.
sooss-pen-SAW-ryohss.

811. Sweater.   Um suéter.   *ōo SWEH-tehr.*

812. Trousers.   Calças (de homem).
KAHL-sahss (day OH-māy).

813. Undershirt.   Uma camisêta.
OO-mah kah-mee-ZAY-tah.

814. Underwear.   Roupa interior.
ROH-pah een-teh-RYOHR.

815. Vest.   Um colête.   *oo koh-LAY-teh.*

HEALTH
A SÁUDE

Accidents.   Os Acidentes.

See also ILLNESS, p. 95.

818. There has been an accident.
Houve um acidente.
OH-vay oo ah-see-DEN-tay.

819. Get a doctor, (nurse) please.
Chame um médico, (uma enfermeira) por
favor.
SHAH-may oo MEH-dee-koh, OO-mah (en-fehr-NAY-rah), pohr fah-VOHR.

820. Send for an ambulance.
Chame uma ambulância.
SHAH-may OO-mah ahm-boo-LAHN-syah.

821. Please bring blankets.
Traga cobertores, por favor.
TRAH-gah koh-behr-TOH-rayss, pohr fah-VOHR.

822. A stretcher, water.
Uma máca, água.
OO-mah MAH-kah, AH-gwah.

823. He is (seriously) hurt.
Êle está (gravemente) ferido.
AY-lay ess-TAH (grah-vay-MEN-tay) fay-REE-doh).

824. Help me carry him.
Ajude-me a carregá-lo.
ah-ZHOO-day-may ah kah-rray-GAH-loh.

825. He was knocked down.
Êle foi atropelado.
AY-lay foy ah-traw-peh-LAH-doh.

826. She has fallen (fainted).
Ela caíu (desmaiou).
EH-lah cah-YEW (dayss-mah-YOH).

827. I feel faint.
Estou desmaiando.
ess-TOH dayss-mah-YAHN-doh.

828. He has a (fracture, bruise, cut).
Tem (uma fratura, uma contusão, um golpe).
ta͞y (OO-mah frah-TOO-rah, OO-mah kohn-too-Z͞OW, o͞o GAWL-pay).

829. He has burned his hand.
Êle queimou a mão.
AY-lay kay-MOH ah mo͞w.

830. It is (bleeding, swollen).
Está (sangrando, inchado).
ess-TAH (sahn-GRAHN-doh, een-SHAH-doh).

831. Can you dress this?
Pode fazer um curativo?
PAW-day fah-ZEHR oo koo-rah-TEE-voh?

832. Have you (any bandages, a splint)?
Tem ataduras, talas)?
tay (ah-tah-DOO-rahss, TAH-lahss)?

833. I need something for a tourniquet.
Preciso de algo para torniquete.
pray-SEE-zoh day AHL-goh PAH-rah tohr-nee-KEH-tay.

834. Are you all right?
Sente-se bem?
SEN-tay-say bay?

835. It hurts here.
Dói aquí.
doy ah-KEE.

836. I want to sit down a moment.
Quero sentar um momento.
KEH-roh sen-TAHR oo moh-MEN-toh.

837. I cannot move my ——.
Não posso mover meu ——.
now PAW-soh moh-VEHR MAY‿oo ——.

838. I have hurt my ——.
Ferí meu ——.
feh-REE MAY‿oo ——.

See PARTS OF THE BODY, p. 105.

839. Can I travel on Monday?

Posso viajar segunda-feira?

PAW-soh vyah-ZHAR say-GOON-dah-FAY-rah?

840. Please notify (my husband, my wife).

Faça o favor de avisar (meu marido, minha espôsa).

FAH-sah oh fah-VOHR day ah-vee-ZAHR (MAY‿oo mah-REE-doh, MEE-nyah (ess-POH-zah).

841. Here is my identification (folder).

Aquí está a minha (carteira de) identidade.

ah-KEE ess-TAH ah MEE-nyah (kahr-TAY-rah day) ee-den-tee-DAH-day.

ILLNESS

AS DOENÇAS

See also ACCIDENTS, p. 92.

844. I wish to see a doctor.

Desejo ver um médico.

day-ZAY-zhoh vehr oo MEH-dee-koh.

845. A specialist, an American doctor.

Um especialista, um médico americano.

oo ess-peh-syah-LEESS-tah, oo MEH-dee-koh ah-may-ree-KAH-noh.

846. I do not sleep well.

Não durmo bem.

now DOOR-moh bay.

847. My foot hurts.
Meu pé está doendo.
MAY-oo peh ess-TAH doh-EN-doh.

848. My head aches.
Tenho dôr de cabêça.
TAY-nyoh dohr day kah-BAY-sah.

See PARTS OF THE BODY, p. 105.

849. I have an abscess.
Tenho um abcesso.
TAY-nyoh o͞o ahb-SEH-soh.

850. Appendicitis, biliousness.
Apendicite, biliosidade.
ah-pen-dee-SEE-tay, bee-lyoh-see-DAH-day.

851. A bite (insect), a blister.
Uma picada (de inséto), uma bôlha.
OO-mah pee-KAH-dah (day een-SEH-toh), OO-mah BOHL-yah.

852. A boil, a burn.
Uma puztema, uma queimadura.
OO-mah pooz-TAY-mah, OO-mah kay-mah-DOO-rah.

853. Chills, a cold.
Calafrios, um resfriado.
kah-lah-FREE-ohss, o͞o rayss-free-AH-doh.

854. Constipation, a cough.
Prisão de ventre, uma tosse.
pree-ZOW day VEN-tray, OO-mah TAW-say.

855. A cramp.
    Uma caimbra.
    OO-mah KAH-eem-brah.

856. Diarrhœa, dysentery.
    Diarréa, disenteria.
    dee-ah-RREH-ah, dee-zen-teh-REE-ah.

857. Earache, fever.
    Dôr de ouvido, febre.
    dohr day oh-VEE-doh, FEH-bray.

858. Food poisoning, a headache.
    Envenenamento, dôr de cabêça.
    en-veh-neh-nah-MEN-toh, dohr day kah-BAY-sah.

859. Hoarseness, indigestion.
    Rouquidão, indigestão.
    roh-kee-D$\overline{OW}$, een-dee-zhehss-T$\overline{OW}$.

860. Nausea, pneumonia.
    Nausea, pneumonia.
    NOW-zeh-ah, pay-neh-oo-maw-NEE-ah.

861. A sore throat, a sprain.
    Inflamação de garganta, uma torcedura.
    een-flah-mah-S$\overline{OW}$ day gahr-GAHN-tah, OO-mah tohr-say-DOO-rah.

862. A sting, a sunburn.
    Uma picada, queimadura de sol.
    OO-mah pee-KAH-dah, kay-mah-DOO-rah day sawl.

863. Sunstroke, typhoid fever.

Insolação, febre tifóide.

een-saw-lah-SŌW, FEH-bray tee-FOY-day.

864. Vomiting.

Vômitos.

VOH-mee-tohss.

865. What am I to do?

Que devo fazer?

kay DAY-voh fah-ZEHR?

866. Must I stay in bed?

Devo ficar na cama?

DAY-voh fee-KAHR na KAH-mah?

867. Do I have to go to the hospital?

Tenho que ir para o hospital?

TAY-nyoh kay eer PAH-rah oh awss-pee-TAHL?

868. May I get up?

Posso levantar-me?

PAW-soh leh-vahn-TAHR-may?

869. I feel better.

Sinto-me melhor.

SEEN-toh-may mehl-YOHR.

870. When do you think I'll be better?

Quando pensa que vou melhorar?

KWAHN-doh PEN-sah kay voh mehl-yoh-RAHR?

871. When will you come again?
Quando virá outra vez?
KWAHN-doh vee-RAH OH-trah vayss?

872. A drop (liquid).
Uma gota.
OO-mah GOH-tah.

873. A tablespoonful, a teaspoonful.
Uma colher de sôpa, uma colher de chá.
OO-mah kohl-YEHR day SOH-pah, OO-mah kohl-YEHR day shah.

874. Every hour (three hours).
De hora em hora (de três em três horas).
day OH-rah $\overline{ay}$ OH-rah (day trayss $\overline{ay}$ trayss OH-rahss).

875. Before (after) meals.
Antes (depois) das refeições.
AHN-tayss (day-POYSS) dahss ray-fay-SOYSS.

876. Twice a day.
Duas veses ao dia.
DOO-ahss VAY-zehss ow DEE-ah.

877. On going to bed, on getting up.
Ao deitar-se, ao levantar-se.
ow day-TAHR-say, ow leh-vahn-TAHR-say.

878. X-ray.
A radiografia.
ah rah-dyoh-grah-FEE-ah.

See also DRUGSTORE, p. 101.

DENTIST
O DENTISTA

881. Where is there a good dentist?
Onde há um bom dentista?
OHN-day ah oo boh den-TEESS-tah?

882. This front (back) tooth hurts.
Êste dente de frente (de trás) me dói.
*AYSS-tay DEN-tay day FREN-tay (day trahss)
may doy.*

883. Can you fix it (temporarily)?
Pode consertá-lo (temporariamente)?
*PAW-day kohn-sehr-TAH-loh (tem-poh-rah-
ryah-MEN-tay)?*

884. I have lost a filling.
Perdí uma obturação.
pehr-DEE OO-mah awb-too-rah-SOW.

885. I have broken a tooth.
Quebrei um dente.
kay-BRAY oo DEN-tay.

886. I do (not) want it extracted.
(Não) quero extraí-lo.
(now) KEH-roh ayss-trah-EE-loh.

887. Can you repair this denture?
Pode consertar esta dentadura?
*PAW-day kohn-sehr-TAHR ESS-tah den-tah-
DOO-rah?*

888. Local anesthetic.
A anestesia local.
ah ah-nehs-teh-ZEE-ah loh-KAHL.

DRUGSTORE
DROGARIA

891. Where is a drugstore where they speak English?

Onde há uma drogaria onde se fale inglês?

OHN-day ah OO-mah draw-gah-REE-ah OHN-day say FAH-lay een-GLAYSS?

892. Can you fill this prescription?

Pode aviar esta receita?

PAW-day ah-VYAHR ESS-tah ray-SAY-tah?

893. How long will it take?

Quanto tempo levará?

KWAHN-toh TEM-poh leh-vah-RAH?

894. I want adhesive tape.

Quero esparadrapo.

KEH-roh ess-pah-rah-DRAH-poh.

895. Alcohol.

Álcool.

AHL-kohl

896. Analgesic.

O analgésico.

oh ah-nahl-GEH-zee-koh.

897. An antiseptic, an aspirin.

Um antisséptico, uma aspirina.

o͞o ahn-tee-SEH-tee-koh, OO-mah ahss-pee-REE-nah.

898. Bandages, bicarbonate of soda.
Ataduras, bicarbonato de soda.
ah-tah-DOO-rahss, bee-kahr-boh-NAH-toh day SAW-dah.

899. Boric acid.
Ácido bórico.
AH-see-doh BAW-ree-koh.

900. A brush (hair, tooth).
Uma escôva (de cabêlo, de dente).
OO-mah ess-KOH-vah (day kah-BAY-loh, day DEN-tay).

901. Carbolic acid, castor oil.
Ácido fênico, óleo de rícino.
AH-see-doh FAY-nee-koh, AW-lay-oh day REE-see-noh.

902. Cleaning fluid.
Tira-manchas.
tee-rah-MAHN-shass.

903. Cold cream.
Crême de limpeza.
KRAY-may day leem-PAY-zah.

904. A comb.
Um pente.
oo PEN-tay.

905. Corn pads, cotton.
Protetores de calos, algodão.
proh-teh-TOH-rayss day KAH-lohss, ahl-goh-DOW.

906. A deodorant.

Um desodorante.

$\overline{oo}$ *day-zoh-doh-RAHN-tay.*

907. Ear stoppers.

Algodão para tampar os ouvidos.

al-gah-D$\overline{OW}$ PAH-rah tahm-PAHR ohss oh-VEE-dohss.

908. Foot powder.

Pó antissético para os pés.

paw ahn-tee-SEH-tee-koh PAH-rah ohs pehss.

909. Gauze, hair tonic.

Gaze, loção para cabêlo.

GAH-zay, loh-S$\overline{OW}$ PAH-rah kah-BAY-loh.

910. A hot water bottle, an ice bag.

Uma bolsa dágua quente, uma bolsa de gêlo.

OO-mah BOHL-sah DAH-gwah KEN-tay, OO-mah BOHL-sah day ZHAY-loh.

911. Insect bite (lotion), insect repellent.

Picada de inséto (loção), inseticida.

pee-KAH-dah day een-SEH-toh (loh-S$\overline{OW}$), een-seh-tee-SEE-dah.

912. Iodine, a laxative.

Iodo, um laxante.

YOH-doh, $\overline{oo}$ lah-SHAN-tay.

913. A lipstick, a medicine dropper.

Um baton, um conta-gotas.

$\overline{oo}$ *bah-T$\overline{OH}$, $\overline{oo}$ kohn-tah-GOH-tahss.*

914. Mercurochrome, a mouth wash.

Mercúrio-cromo, um gargarejo.

mehr-KOO-ryoh-KROH-moh, $\overline{oo}$ gahr-gah-RAY-zhoh.

915. Poison.

O veneno.

oh vay-NAY-noh.

916. Peroxide, powder, quinine.

Água oxigenada, pó, quinino.

AH-gwah awk-see-zhay-NAH-dah, paw, kee-NEE-noh.

917. A safety razor, razor blades.

Uma máquina de barbear, giletes.

OO-mah MAH-kee-nah day bahr-bay-AHR, zhee-LEH-tayss.

918. Rouge.

Rouge.

ROO-zhay.

919. Sanitary napkins, a sedative.

Toalhas higiênicas (Modess), um sedativo.

TWAHL-yahss ee-zhee-AY-nee-kahss (MAW-dess), $\overline{oo}$ seh-dah-TEE-voh.

920. Shampoo (creme, liquid).

Shampú (creme, líquido).

shahm-POO (KRAY-may, LEE-kee-doh).

921. Shaving cream (lotion).

Creme de barbear (loção).

KRAY-may day bahr-bay-AHR (loh-SŌW).

922. Soap, sunburn ointment.
Sabonête, unguento para queimadura de sol.

sah-boh-NAY-tay, oon-GWEN-toh PAH-rah kay-mah-DOO-rah day sawl.

923. Sun tan lotion.
Loção contra queimadura do sol.

loh-SOW KOHN-trah kay-mah-DOO-rah doh sawl.

924. A thermometer (for fever).
Um termômetro (para febre).

oo tehr-MOH-meh-troh (PAH-rah FEH-bray)

925. Tooth (paste, powder).
(Pasta, pó) de dente.

(PAHSS-tah, paw) day DEN-tay.

PARTS AND ORGANS OF BODY
PARTES E ORGÃOS DO CORPO

926. The ear. O ouvido. *oh oh-VEE-doh.*

927. The eye. O ôlho. *oh OHL-yoh.*

928. The face. O rosto. *oh ROHSS-toh.*

929. The finger. O dedo. *oh DAY-doh.*

930. The foot. O pé. *oh peh.*

931. The hand. A mão. *ah mow.*

932. The head. A cabêça. *ah kah-BAY-sah.*

933. The leg. A perna. *ah PEHR-nah.*

934. The mouth. A bôca. *ah BOH-kah.*

935. The nose. O nariz. *oh nah-REES.*

COMMUNICATIONS
COMUNICAÇÕES

Telephone. Telefone.

See NUMBERS, p. 113.

986. Where may I telephone?
Onde posso telefonar?
OHN-day PAW-soh teh-lay-foh-NAHR?

987. Will you telephone for me?
Quer telefonar para mim?
kehr teh-lay-foh-NAHR PAH-rah mēe?

988. I want to make a local call to ——.
Quero fazer uma chamada para ——.
KEH-roh fah-ZEHR OO-mah shah-MAH-dah PAH-rah ——.

989. A long distance call.
Uma chamada interurbana.
OO-mah shah-MAH-dah een-tehr-oor-BAH-nah.

990. The operator will call you.
A telefonista chamará.
ah teh-lay-foh-NEES-tah shah-mah-RAH.

991. I want number ——.
Quero número ——.
KEH-roh NOO-may-roh ——.

992. Hello (on the telephone).
Alô.
ah-LOH.

993. They do not answer.
Não respondem.
now rayss-POHN-day.

994. The line is busy.
A linha está ocupada.
ah LEE-nyah ess-TAH oh-koo-PAH-dah.

995. Dial it again.
Disque outra vez.
DEES-kay OH-trah vayss.

996. May I speak to ——?
Posso falar com ——?
PAW-soh fah-LAH koh ——?

997. He is not in.
Êle não está.
AY-lay now ess-TAH.

998. This is —— speaking.
Aquí fala ——.
ah-KEE FAH-lah ——.

999. Please take a message for ——.
Faça o favôr de dar um recado para ——.
FAH-sah oh fah-VOHR day dahr oo reh-KAH-doh PAH-rah ——.

1000. My number is ——.
Meo número é ——.
MAY_oo NOO-may-roh eh ——.

1001. How much is a call to ——?
Quanto custa uma chamada para ——?
KWAHN-toh KOOSS-tah OO-mah shah-MAH-dah PAH-rah ——?

1002. You have a telephone call.

Chamam-lhe ao telefone.

SHAH-mah-yay ow teh-lay-FOH-nay.

Telegrams and Cablegrams.   Telegramas
e cabogramas

**1003. Where can I send (a telegram, a
cable)?**

Onde posso mandar (um telegrama, um
cabograma)?

*OHN-day PAW-soh mahn-DAHR oo teh-
lay-GRAH-mah (oo kah-boh-GRAH-mah)?*

1004. What is the rate a word to ——?

Quanto custa a palavra para ——?

*KWAHN-toh KOOSS-tah ah pah-LAH-
vrah PAH-rah ——?*

1005. Where are the forms?

Onde estão os formulários?

*OHN-day ess-TOW ohss fohr-moo-LAH-
ryohss?*

1006. Urgent, collect.

Urgente, a cobrar.

oor-ZHEN-tay, ah koh-BRAHR.

1007. When will it arrive?

Quando chegará?

KWAHN-doh sheh-gah-RAH?

1008. I wish to pay for the answer.

Desejo com resposta paga.

*day-ZAY-zhoh koh rayss-PAWSS-tah PAH-
gah.*

USEFUL INFORMATION
INFORMAÇÕES UTEIS

Days of the Week.   Dias da semana

1011. Monday, Tuesday.
Segunda-feira, terça-feira.
say-GOON-dah-FAY-rah, TEHR-sah-FAY-rah.

1012. Wednesday, Thursday.
Quarta-feira, quinta-feira.
KWAHR-tah-FAY-rah, KEEN-tah-FAY-rah.

1013. Friday, Saturday.
Sexta-feira, sábado.
SESS-tah-FAY-rah, SAH-bah-doh.

1014. Sunday.
Domingo.
doh-MEEN-goh.

Months and Seasons.   Meses e estações.

1015. January, February.
Janeiro, fevereiro.
zhah-NAY-roh, feh-vay-RAY-roh.

1016. March, April.
Março, abril.
MAHR-soh, ah-BREEL.

1017. May, June.
Maio, junho.
MAH-yoh, ZHOO-nyoh.

1018. July, August.
Julho, agôsto.
ZHOOL-yoh, ah-GOHSS-toh.

1019. September, October.
Setembro, outubro.
seh-TEM-broh, oh-TOO-broh.

1020. November, December.
Novembro, dezembro.
noh-VEM-broh, deh-ZEM-broh.

1021. Spring, Summer.
A primavera, o verão.
ah pree-mah-VEH-rah, oh veh-ROW.

1022. Autumn, Winter.
O outono, o inverno.
oh oh-TOH-noh, oh een-VEHR-noh.

Weather. Tempo.

1023. It is (warm, cold) (weather).
Faz (calor, frio).
fahss (kah-LOHR, FREE-oh).

1024. It is (fair, good, bad).
O tempo está (claro, bom, mau).
oh TEM-poh ess-TAH (KLAH-roh, boh, mow).

1025. It is (raining, drizzling).
Está (chovendo, garoando).   [*doh*].
ess-TAH (shoh-VEN-doh, gah-roh-AHN-

1026. The sun, sunny, shady.
O sol, ensolarado, nublado.   [*doh.*
oh sawl, en-saw-loh-RAH-doh, noo-BLAH-

Time and Time Expressions. A hora.

1027. What time is it?
Que horas são?
kay OH-rahss sow?

1028. It is one o'clock.
É uma hora.
eh OO-mah OH-rah.

1029. It is half past five.
São cinco e meia.
sow SEEN-koh ee MAY-yah.

1030. It is a quarter past five.
São cinco horas e um quarto.
sow SEEN-koh OH-rahss ee oo KWAHR-toh.

1031. It is a quarter to six.
Falta um quarto para as seis.
FAHL-tah oo KWAHR-toh PAH-rah ahss sayss.

1032. At ten past seven (in the morning).
Às sete e dez (da manhã).
ahss SEH-tay ee dehss (dah mah-NYAH).

1033. At ten to nine (in the evening).
Às dez para as nove (da noite).
ahss dehss PAH-rah ahss NAW-vay (dah NOY-tay).

1034. It is late.
É tarde.
eh TAHR-day.

1035. In the (morning, evening).
De (manhã, noite).
day (mah-NYĀH, NOY-tay).

1036. In the afternoon.
De tarde.
day TAHR-day.

1037. At noon, at midnight.
Ao meio-dia, à meia-noite.
ow MAY-yoh-DEE-ah, ah MAY-yah-NOY-tay.

1038. Day. Night.
O dia. A noite.
oh DEE-ah. ah NOY-tay.

1039. Yesterday, last night.
Ôntem, ôntem à noite.
OHN-tay, OHN-tay ah NOY-tay.

1040. Today, tonight.
Hoje, hoje à noite.
OH-zhay, OH-zhay ah NOY-tay.

1041. Tomorrow.
Amanhã.
ah-mah-NYĀH.

1042. (The) day before yesterday.
Anteontem.
ahn-tay-OHN-tay.

1043. Last year (month).
O ano (mês) passado.
oh AH-noh (mayss) pah-SAH-doh.

1044. Last Monday.
Segunda-feira passada.
say-GOON-dah-FAY-rah pah-SAH-dah.

1045. Next week.
Na próxima semana.
nah PRAWS-see-mah say-MAH-nah.

1046. Two weeks ago.
Há duas semanas.
ah DOO-ahss say-MAH-nahss.

1047. NUMBERS
NÚMEROS

One. Um. $\overline{oo}$.

Two. Dois. *doyss.*

Three. Três. *trayss.*

Four. Quatro. *KWAH-troh.*

Five. Cinco. *SEEN-koh.*

Six. Seis. *sayss.*

Seven. Sete. *SEH-tay.*

Eight. Oito. *OY-toh.*

Nine. Nove. *NAW-vay.*

Ten. Dez. *dehss.*

Eleven. Onze. *OHN-zay.*

Twelve. Doze. *DOH-zay.*

Thirteen. Treze. *TRAY-zay.*

Fourteen. Catorze. *kah-TOHR-zay.*

Fifteen. Quinze. *KEEN-zay.*

Sixteen. Dezeseis. *deh-zay-SAYSS.*

Seventeen. Dezesete. *deh-zay-SEH-tay.*

Eighteen. Dezoito. *deh-ZOY-toh.*

Nineteen. Dezenove. *deh-zay-NAW-vay.*

Twenty. Vinte. *VEEN-tay.*

Twenty-one. Vinte e um. *VEEN-tee oo.*

Twenty-two. Vinte e dois. *VEEN-tee doyss.*

Thirty. Trinta. *TREEN-tah.*

Thirty-one. Trinta e um. *TREEN-tah ee oo.*

Forty. Quarenta. *kwah-REN-tah.*

Fifty. Cinquenta. *seen-KWEN-tah.*

Sixty. Sessenta. *say-SEN-tah.*

Seventy. Setenta. *say-TEN-tah.*

Eighty. Oitenta. *oy-TEN-tah.*

Ninety. Noventa. *noh-VEN-tah.*

One hundred. Cem. *say.*

One hundred and one. Cento e um.
SEN-toh ee oo.

Two hundred. Duzentos. *doo-ZEN-tohss.*

Three hundred. Trezentos. *tray-ZEN-tohss.*

Four hundred. Quatrocentos. *kwah-troh-SEN-tohss.*

Five hundred. Quinhentos. *kee-NYEN-tohss.*

Six hundred. Seiscentos. *sayss-SEN-tohss.*

Seven hundred. Setecentos. *seh-tay-SEN-tohss.*

Eight hundred. Oitocentos. *oy-toh-SEN-tohss.*

Nine hundred. Novecentos. *naw-vay-SEN-tohss.*

One thousand. Mil. *meel.*

First. Primeiro. *pree-MAY-roh.*

Second. Segundo. *say-GOON-doh.*

Third. Terceiro. *tehr-SAY-roh.*

Fourth. Quarto. *KWAHR-toh.*

Fifth. Quinto. *KEEN-toh.*

Sixth. Sexto. *SAYSS-toh.*

Seventh. Sétimo. *SEH-tee-moh.*

Eighth. Oitavo. *oy-TAH-voh.*

Ninth. Nono. *NOH-noh.*

Tenth. Décimo. *DEH-see-moh.*

MEASUREMENTS
AS MEDIDAS

1050. What is the length, width?

Qual é o comprimento, a largura?

kwahl eh oh kohm-pree-MEN-toh, ah lahr-GOO-rah?

1051. How much per meter?

Quanto custa o metro?

KWAHN-toh KOOSS-tah oh MEH-troh?

1052. What is the size?

De que tamanho é?

day kay tah-MAN-nyoh eh?

1053. It is ten meters long, by four meters.

Tem dez metros de comprimento, por quatro metros de largura.

tay dehss MEH-trohss day kohm-pree-MEN-toh pohr KWAH-troh MEH-trohss day lahr-GOO-rah.

1054. High, low.

Alto, baixo.

AHL-toh, BIE-shoh.

1055. Large, small, medium.

Grande, pequeno, médio.

GRAHN-day, pay-KAY-noh, MEH-dyoh.

1056. Alike, different.

Parecido, diferente.

pah-ray-SEE-doh, dee-fay-REN-tay.

1057. A pair, dozen.

Um par, uma dúzia.

oo pahr, OO-mah DOO-zyah.

1058. Half a dozen.
Meia dúzia.
MAY-yah DOO-zyah.

1059. Half a meter.
Meio metro.
MAY-yoh MEH-troh.

COLORS
CÔRES

1062. Light, dark.
Claro, escuro.
KLAH-roh, ess-KOO-roh.

1063. Black, blue, brown.
Preto, azul, marron.
PRAY-toh, ah-ZOOL, mah-RRŌH.

1064. Cream, gray, green.
Crême, cinzento, verde.
KRAY-may, seen-ZEN-toh, VAYR-day.

1065. Orange, pink, purple.
Laranja, rosado, roxo.
lah-RAHN-zhah, roh-ZAH-doh, ROH-zhoh.

1066. Red, white.
Vermelho, branco.
vehr-MEHL-yoh, BRAHN-koh.

1067. Yellow.
Amarelo.
ah-mah-REH-loh.

COMMON OBJECTS
OBJETOS COMUNS

1070. Ash tray. O cinzeiro. *oh seen-ZAY-roh.*

1071. Bag. A bolsa. *ah BOHL-sah.*

1072. Bobby pins. Os grampos. *ohss GRAHM-pohss.*

1073. Box. A caixa. *ah KIE-shah.*

1074. Bulb (light). A lâmpada. *ah LAHM-pah-dah.*

1075. Candy. Bombons. *bohm-BOHSS.*

1076. Can opener. O abridor de latas. *oh ah-bree-DOHR day LAH-tahss.*

1077. Cloth (cotton, linen, rayon, silk, wool).
A fazenda (algodão, linho, rayon, sêda, lã).
ah fah-ZEN-dah (ahl-goh-DŌW, LEE-nyoh, rah-YŌH, SAY-dah, lah).

1078. Corkscrew. O saca-rolha. *oh sah-kah-ROHL-yah.*

1079. Corsage. O corsage. *oh kohr-SAH-zhay.*

1080. Cushion. A almofada. *ah ahl-moh-FAH-dah.*

1081. Doll. A boneca. *ah boh-NEH-kah.*

1082. Earring. O brinco. *oh BREEN-koh.*

1083. Flashlight. A lanterna. *ah lahn-TEHR-nah.*

1084. Glasses (sun). Os óculos (escuros).
ohss AW-koo-lohss (ess-KOO-rohss).

1085. Gold. O ouro. *oh OH-roh.*

1086. Chewing gum. O chiclete. *oh SHEE-kleh-tay.*

1087. Hairnet. A rêde de cabêlo.
ah RAY-day day kah-BAY-loh.

1088. Hairpin. O grampo de cabêlo.
oh GRAHM-poh day kah-BAY-loh.

1089. Hook. O gancho. *oh GAHN-shoh.*

1090. Iron (flat). O ferro. *oh FEH-rroh.*

1091. Jewelry (jewels). As jóias. *ahss ZHAW-yahss.*

1092. Lace (shoe). O cordão de sapato.
oh kohr-DŌW (day sah-PAH-toh).

1093. Leather. O couro. *oh KOH-roh.*

1094. Mending cotton. O algodão de serzir.
oh ahl-goh-DŌW day sehr-ZEER.

1095. Mosquito net. O mosquiteiro.
oh mohss-kee-TAY-roh.

1096. Nail file. A lima de unhas.
ah LEE-mah day OO-nyahss.

1097. Necklace. O colar. *oh koh-LAHR.*

1098. Needle. A agulha. *ah ah-GOOL-yah.*

1099. Perfume. O perfume. *oh pehr-FOO-may.*

1100. Pin (ornamental). O broche. *oh BROH-shay.*

1101. Pin (straight). O alfinete. *oh ahl-fee-NAY-tay.*

1102. Radio. O radio. *oh RAH-dyoh.*

1103. Ring. O anel. *oh ah-NEHL.*

1104. Rubbers. As galochas. *ahss gah-LAW-shahss.*

1105. Safety pin. O alfinete de segurança.
oh ahl-fee-NAY-tay day say-goo-RAHN-sah.

1106. Scissors. A tesoura. *ah tay-ZOH-rah.*

1107. Silver. A prata. *ah PRAH-tah.*

1108. Stone (precious). A pedra (preciosa).
ah PEH-drah (pray-SYOH-zah).

1109. Stopper. A tampa. *ah TAHM-pah.*

1110. Strap. A correia. *ah koh-RRAY-yah.*

1111. Straw. A palha. *ah PAHL-yah.*

1112. Thimble. O dedal. *oh day-DAHL.*

1113. Thread. O fio. *oh FEE-oh.*

1114. Toy. O brinquedo. *oh breen-KAY-doh.*

1115. Typewriter. A máquina de escrever.
ah MAH-kee-nah day ess-kray-VEHR.

1116. Umbrella. O guardachuva.
ah gwahr-dah-SHOO-vah.

1117. Vase. O vaso. *oh VAH-zoh.*

1118. Wash cloth. O esfregão. *oh ess-fray-GOW.*

1119. Watch (wrist). O relógio (de pulso).
oh ray-LAW-zhoh (day POOL-soh).

1120. Whiskbroom. A escôva de roupa.
ah ess-KOH-vah day ROH-pah.

1121. Wood. A madeira. *ah mah-DAY-rah.*

1122. Wool (mending). A lã de serzir.
ah lah day sehr-ZEER.

1123. Zipper. O zip. *oh ZEE-pay.*

INDEX

The words in capitals refer to sections, and the first number that follows (example : p. 46) refers to the page. Otherwise ALL ENTRIES ARE INDEXED BY ITEM NUMBER.